CARP FISH
(A YEAR IN FRANCE)

Steve Graham

Published in 2015 by FeedARead.com Publishing

Copyright © The author as named on the book cover.

First Edition

A CIP catalogue record for this title is available from the British Library.

INDEX

To all the wonderful friends that I have met during my time in France -

Benoit, Corentin, Clément, Vincent, Alexi, Dupont and many more too numerous to mention.

You have made my visits so very special, and I can't thank you all enough.

CHAPTER ONE - CONTRE

After my last trip to Picardie in October 2014, I realised that I wouldn`t get a chance to go back to France until the following spring, but I fully intended to have a few sessions during the winter on one or two English lakes. I knew that Woodland Waters had fished very well the previous winter, and I had always enjoyed my time fishing there, but there were a couple of other lakes nearby that I thought I might try too. I went on holiday to Lanzarote with my wife Anita in November and when we got back the weather wasn`t very good, so I decided to postpone the next fishing trip for a while, and take the chance to do a bit more writing. Before I knew it, Christmas was upon us and I still hadn`t been. We travelled down to Portsmouth to spend a few days with my dad just after the new year, and when we got back, I still didn`t get the rods out.

In February I started to make plans to fish in France again. I rang Vincent and arranged to fish on one of his lakes at Contre for four days, and I decided to follow that with four days on one of the back lakes at Loeuilly. Not fishing for four months certainly hadn`t been my intention, but in a way it did me a favour because it gave me time to recharge the batteries, as it were, and I was now absolutely gagging to get the rods out again.

I had fished the first lake at Contre just twice the previous year, and I hadn`t been very successful there. I caught three sturgeon on my first session there, and my second visit produced three more sturgeon and just one small common, but the big mirrors that the lake contained eluded me completely. It`s strange because this was meant to be the easiest of Vincent`s two lakes, but I had done really well every time that I`d fished on the middle lake, which was reputed to be very difficult.

That's fishing I suppose.

I don't like being beaten however, and I had one or two ideas that I thought might work on the first lake. One idea was to use bread-crumbs in little sticks attached to the hook-bait, and another was to bait heavily with peanuts on one rod. Tigernuts were a very successful bait there, but a lot of anglers were using them. Peanuts however had not been used on the lake for a long time, if at all, and I thought that they might just be the edge that I needed. The only thing that worried me about using peanuts there was the water temperature. I have usually found that peanuts don't work quite so well in cold water conditions because the oils aren't released from the nuts so much. They seem to work much better in warmer water. I was due to fish at Contre in the second week of March, so I had a real concern that the water would not have warmed up enough, but I thought that I'd try anyway. Perhaps I could bait up one spot heavily with the peanuts, and not fish it initially. I could just keep an eye on the area and if I saw any signs of fish, I could reposition a rod to fish there. If I didn't see any signs of fish over the peanuts, then I hadn't done any harm anyway. I was much more confident that my idea of using bread crumbs in sticks would work. This has been a successful method for me on many occasions, in all sorts of conditions, and the low water temperature wouldn't harm that method.

In the couple of weeks before I was due to leave, I tied up rigs, re-spooled my reels with new line and stocked up with leads and other various essentials. All the boilies were air-dried, so that they'd last the full eight days of the trip. Hemp, tigers and peanuts were prepared and frozen, and the white bread that I was going to use was put through the blender to turn it into bread-crumbs, and then dried thoroughly. I can't remember the last time that I was so well prepared for a fishing trip, and I just hoped that all that effort would be rewarded with some good fish.

The last few days really dragged, but eventually it was time to load the car. That wasn`t as easy as normal, because I had a lot of extra tackle to take with me. My friend Corentin had asked me to take a lot of things to France for him. He had bought these from eBay, but they couldn`t be delivered to France, so they were sent to me instead, and I would then give them to Corentin when I got to Contre. Corentin had ordered a new sleeping bag, a bed-chair cover, a bivvy table, three carry-alls and several more things besides, so with all of my tackle and bait in the car too, there wasn`t much room. Fortunately it all went in somehow, but it certainly was a bit of a squeeze.

I finally left home just after half past eight on the Wednesday night. During the drive down the motorway to Dover I listened to the football on the radio, and Chelsea somehow managed to snatch defeat out of the jaws of victory, when they were knocked out of the champions league by Paris St. Germain on away goals. Paris had played the last hour with only ten men after Zlatan Ibrahimovic was sent off, but they still managed to score two goals and knock Chelsea out.

There were a few 50 m.p.h. sections of the M1 due to road works, but nothing too bad, although it seemed as though everywhere else was grinding to a halt. I drove past signs telling me that the M4 was shut, then the M3 was shut, The A2 and then the A1 were shut too. It was almost getting to the stage where it would have been easier to list the roads that weren`t shut. Despite all of that, I made good progress, and I arrived at Dover about one and a half hours before my check-in time. Luckily, the nice man in the P & O check-in box allowed me to get on an earlier ferry, so I was soon on board and on my way to France.

The crossing went without a hitch, and I started out on the two hour drive to Contre. When I was about half-way there, I glanced at the temperature gauge which read 4 degrees. Now that was colder than I would have liked, but the lake was a fair bit further south, so I hoped that it might be a couple of degrees warmer there. Unfortunately that wasn`t the case, and when I drove through the gate at the entrance to the lake at just before half past six in the morning, the temperature gauge was now reading -2 degrees and the ground was covered with a thick layer of white frost. None of the weather forecasts that I had looked at before I came had predicted that, and my confidence took a big dip when I saw how cold it was.

In those conditions, the first thing that I did was to put on some warm clothes – a thick coat with a thermal lining, leggings and a woolly hat. Next I set up the bivvy and made myself comfortable and put the kettle on for a nice warm cup of tea. Unbelievably, just a couple of hours or so later the scene was completely different. The sun was shining out of cloudless blue sky, and it started to feel rather pleasant. The frost melted and the temperature rose to the heady heights of ten degrees, but of course the water was still very cold indeed.

I got out my marker rod and I soon found five really nice spots for the rods. I was only going to use four rods, but by baiting five spots, it meant that there was always one baited area without any lines going through it. Hopefully this would help to build up the carps' confidence and get one or two of them to make a mistake. After I`d baited up the spots, I left them for two or three hours before I started fishing. Once again I was trying to build up the fishes' confidence before I made a cast in anger. The spots that I'd found were in several different depths of water. The plan was that if one of those produced a fish for me, then I could look for other spots with the same depth.

Vincent came to see me just after one o'clock that afternoon, and we had a good catch-up. He told me that there was an 'Enduro' (a four-day carp match) at Loeuilly the following month, and he wanted me to fish with him. Now I don't really like carp matches at all. There always seems to be too many people there, who make a lot of noise and disturbance, and the fishing is often dreadful. Vincent seemed very keen to fish the Enduro however, so despite my reservations, I agreed to fish with him.

The afternoon was very uneventful, without a single bleep from my delkims and with no fish sightings at all. I was just thinking about re-casting the rods for the night when Corentin arrived. I gave him all of the tackle that he'd bought from EBay, and he gave me my permit for Albert, where I hoped to fish later in the year. The Albert permit also contained 'Les Timbres' which allowed me to fish on lakes with running water entering them. I would need that when I moved to Loeuilly on Monday. We stood there talking and watching what appeared to be a totally lifeless looking lake, and we both agreed that it was too early in the year, and the water was far too cold. Neither of us expected me to catch very much, if anything, that session.

Corentin left at about five o'clock and his car had barely gone out of the gate when I heard a couple of bleeps from one of my delkims, followed a few seconds later by the indicator rising slowly to the rod. I didn't need telling twice, and when I lifted the rod I found myself doing battle with what seemed to be a very powerful fish. It didn't make any fast runs, but just plodded slowly around and I wasn't able to gain much control at all. The fish moved powerfully to my left and I was forced to follow it down the bank. When I finally got level with the fish, it turned and headed back towards where I had initially hooked it. The battle continued for quite some time, and I still hadn`t even seen the fish, but I was starting to think that it might be a very big carp indeed, and I was just praying that the hook would hold. Eventually I managed to bring the fish towards me and I caught a glimpse of it as it neared the surface. You can imagine my disappointment when I realised that it wasn`t a carp at all, but a sturgeon, and shortly afterwards it was in the net.

Now sturgeon certainly aren`t one of my favourite fish, but at least I had caught something, so maybe a carp or two would follow. I weighed the sturgeon, which stopped the dial at 16 lbs 6 oz, and at least I now knew that I wasn`t going to blank. I was still finding it a little difficult to get over my disappointment however, because while I had been playing the fish I had been sure that it was a carp.

After returning the sturgeon, I re-casted the rods for the night, and re-baited two of the spots. I didn`t put any more bait around the other two because I hadn`t had much action, so I presumed that there was still bait there. I decided to wait and see what the night produced, and then adjust my baiting accordingly in the morning.

Unfortunately, as soon as the sun went down the temperature plummeted, and I was soon tucked up inside my sleeping bag to keep warm. I heard two fish crash out about half an hour after nightfall. I couldn`t see exactly where they were because it was too dark, but they were certainly not too far away from where I was fishing. By the sound that they made as they re-entered the water, they were big fish, which got me quite excited at the time, thinking that I`d got a really good chance. It was not to be however, and it got increasingly colder after that and I didn`t hear any more fish all night.

I did have one occurrence in the early hours of Friday morning. I heard a series of bleeps from the delkim on my third rod. I put on my boots and hurried out of the bivvy to investigate, but when I arrived at the rod the bleeps stopped and the indicator dropped back into position. Thinking that it must have been a liner, I just left it and went back to bed, but when I retrieved the rig in the morning I realised that it hadn`t been a liner at all, because the pop-up was missing and I just retrieved a bare hook. Of course it needn`t have necessarily been a carp that was responsible. It could just as easily have been a rat, of which there are many at this lake, and they often pick up hook-baits, but I couldn`t help but feel that I had missed a chance.

Friday was overcast and cold with an easterly wind which made it feel even colder, and I spent most of the day sat in my bivvy trying to keep warm. Once again I saw no signs of any fish at all and despite trying several variations of rigs and baits, I had no further action to my rods.

Two French anglers arrived just after five o`clock that evening, and they set up half way along the opposite bank. I thought that they were going to fish in my lake, but the Middle Lake is along that side, and they fished there.

About an hour or so later I hooked another fish, but this time it jumped clear of the water just after I`d hooked it and I was left in no doubts that it was another sturgeon. This one weighed just a few ounces less than the first.

The night was cold once again and the lake was flat calm, so I was soon inside my sleeping bag and fast asleep. My dreams were disturbed shortly after ten o`clock that night when I was awakened by a screaming delkim. The fish had

11

picked up my tigernut hook-bait that I had placed in the margin, and when I picked up the rod it powered away from me. I was able to stop the run without too much difficulty, and after that it didn't give me too many problems. I'd caught a glimpse of the fish fairly early on in the fight and realised that it was a carp at last, so I took my time and played it very carefully, but a short while later it was safely within the folds of my net. I left the fish in the net in the margins, with a bank-stick securing the net to the bank, and then I set about organising everything in readiness for weighing the fish. It wasn't a big fish, a mirror carp of eighteen pounds exactly, but I was ecstatic. I'd caught a carp at last, and in such poor conditions it meant a lot to me. I sacked the carp a little further along the margin so that I could get some decent photos in the morning, and after making sure that the fish was happy, I hurried back to the warmth of my sleeping bag.

The following morning I heard a few bleeps from one of my delkims and I hooked a rat that had picked up my left-hand hook-bait. I detest those horrible creatures, but after administering it's just rewards with a bank-stick, I felt a little happier that that particular filthy creature wouldn't be picking up any more of my baits.

Around midday one of the French anglers, who was fishing in the Middle Lake, came to see me. He introduced himself as Kevin, and he seemed to be a very pleasant chap. He couldn't speak a word of English, but we managed to converse in French, and he stayed for about an hour. He told me that neither himself, nor his friend, had caught anything at all in the other lake, which didn't surprise me at all. The Middle Lake holds some superb fish, but it is quite difficult at the best of times, and in these conditions I thought that it would be almost impossible. I planned to fish in that lake at the end of April, but I hoped that by then the weather would have warmed up considerably. Perhaps that would give me the chance to catch some of the superb carp that lived there.

In the afternoon my friend Benoit came to see me and he brought me a beer. He wasn`t very happy because his parents had recently split up, and they were about to get divorced. He was living with his mother during the week, and visiting his father at the week-end. Unfortunately the separation was not very amicable, and Benoit was caught in the middle. We talked all afternoon and I hope that it cheered him up a little.

It was still very cold, which it had been all day, with the sun failing to make an appearance at all. With it being this cold now, I dreaded to think what the night might have in store. The weather forecast predicted rain for the following day, but perhaps that would bring with it a small rise in temperature. I wasn`t quite sure however, which was the worst – The cold or the rain.

On Sunday morning I saw a fish head and shoulder at about thirty yards range in line with a large tree on the far bank, so I re-casted two of my rods. I positioned one hook-bait where I had seen the fish, and the other was casted about ten feet to the right. I then catapulted just half a dozen boilies in the general area and sat back to wait with my fingers crossed.

The take came at twenty past three that afternoon, but it wasn`t on one of my re-casted rods. The fish picked up my left-hand hook-bait, and turned out to be my third sturgeon of the session, which weighed 15 lbs 12 oz.

I retrieved all the rigs at five o`clock that evening, ready to re-cast for the night. Unbelievably, both the rigs that I had casted towards the showing fish were tangled. That was the only two tangles that I had during the whole session, but what a time for it to happen!

That last night was extremely cold with a very hard frost, and I didn't hear a single bleep from the delkims or any sounds of any carp at all. When I woke on Monday morning everything was covered in a thick layer of white frost, just as it had been when I'd arrived, and not surprisingly I had to settle for just the one carp and three sturgeon that I had caught earlier.

It was now time for me to pack up and move to Loeuilly, where I would fish for the next four days. Hopefully I'd fare a little better there.

CHAPTER TWO – LOEUILLY

I arrived at Loeuilly just after eleven o'clock on Monday morning, and my first stop was at 'Le Mairie' to buy my permit, which was 110 euros. That entitled me to fish in all three of the lakes at Loeuilly for the whole calendar year. Now when you consider that all of these lakes contained carp in excess of forty pounds, I thought that was a real bargain. I dread to think what it would cost to fish three lakes of that calibre back in England. After buying my permit, I drove to the supermarket in the nearby village of Conty, where I stocked up with milk, fruit and various other bits and pieces, before driving to the lakes.

I decided not to fish the main lake this time, but to fish one of the two smaller back lakes instead, so I parked the car and had a walk around both lakes. I didn't see any signs of fish, but I preferred the smaller of the two lakes, and I chose a swim about mid-way along the near bank.

The first thing that I did was to set up the bivvy and get everything organised. It felt much warmer and I was soon wearing just a tee-shirt. What a change from the previous day when I had been wrapped up in fleeces, hat and coat, and I was still cold.

Once the bivvy was organised, I picked up the marker rod, and started to try to find some suitable areas to fish to. Normally on this lake, it's a case of trying to find a hole in the weed, but at the end of the previous year they had removed a lot of the weed from all of the lakes here. They use a special weed-cutting machine, attached to a boat, which cuts the weed very close to the lake-bed, and removes it too. It's a marvellous machine, but apparently it is very expensive to hire, so they don't use it very often.

I soon found three lovely areas, all at about thirty yards range, and the lake-bed was so clear that I decided to use my favourite method on all three rods – a light running lead on a fluorocarbon main-line, fished slack.

The left-hand spot was four feet deep and the other two spots were about five feet deep, so as the surrounding area was about a foot shallower, they seemed like a good starting point. I found a nice area for my fourth rod about ten yards short of the far bank, to my right. This was quite a distance to cast, and I wouldn't be able to reach that far with my fluorocarbon line, so I decided to use mono on that rod. I used a swivel lead in a lead-clip rather than the running leads that I was using on the other rods, and I placed a flying back-lead onto the line to try to keep it close to the lakebed in the area around my hook-bait. It was about 6½ feet deep here, which was much deeper than the rest of the lake, and it felt like firm silt, so I had high hopes that it would produce a fish or two for me.

I baited all the spots with just boilies of two different sizes, but the amounts varied. I put 150 boilies on the left-hand spot, 120 on the next and 80 on the third spot. The far bank area was baited the heaviest of all, with 180 boilies being spread around that area. The spot that I was fishing was only about ten yards from the far bank, so it was simplicity itself to just walk around the lake and throw the boilies out by hand. The baiting was finished by about three o'clock, but I decided not to fish straight away. There were two reasons for that decision. The first reason was that I was hungry, because I hadn't had anything to eat since breakfast, but the other reason was that I wanted to leave the swim undisturbed for a while, without any lines in the water. It couldn't do any harm and I wasn't in a hurry, because I had four days in front of me.

My idea about leaving the swim undisturbed didn`t quite work out as planned however, because three ducks appeared and started diving where I had thrown the boilies. Now coots and tufties diving on my baits are annoying, but I often think that ducks are even worse, because they make such a splash when they dive. It certainly wasn`t helping matters and I tried several things to make them leave. I waved the landing net at them, then I chucked an empty spod at them, but nothing seemed to deter them, so in the end I just sat there totally frustrated and called them names.

Unsurprisingly, that didn`t work either.

It was now so warm and sunny that I had to wear a cap and sun-glasses, because it was difficult to see in the bright sun, but the water was still very cold and with a clear sky, the temperature was bound to plummet overnight.

I finally made my first casts at about half past six (an hour before dark) and sat back in my chair to try to relax with a cup of coffee. For the first night I decided to keep things simple, and I put pop-ups on three rods and tigernuts on the fourth. I wasn`t really expecting much to happen on the first night, but you never know.

I woke just after dawn, but it was hard to tell, because there was thick fog. The fog was so dense that I could barely see ten yards. It was also bitterly cold and everything was covered in a coating of thick white frost. That certainly wasn`t what I was hoping for to start the day. I had hoped that the warm sun of the previous day would have raised the water temperature a little, but that had now been completely undone by these conditions, and the water temperature may have actually dropped, and was probably lower now than when I started.

The fog and frost remained until about nine o`clock, and then the fog cleared and the sun came out. There was barely a cloud in the sky, and although it was still very cold, it looked as though it should get warmer, later in the day.

I put the kettle on for the first cup of coffee of the day, but before it had boiled, a series of bleeps from my left-hand rod had me leaping up from my chair and racing towards the rod.

OK perhaps leaping and racing is a bit strong. In reality I lifted my aching back from the chair and walked towards the rod.

When I reached the rod however, my hopes were dashed, when I saw a coot scuttling away from the area looking decidedly guilty. When I retrieved the rig I discovered that the coot had taken the pop-up.

'Oh well,' I thought 'At least something likes my boilies.'

About ten minutes later there was a repeat performance, but to my second rod. This time a duck was responsible, not a coot, and I felt a perverse sense of victory when I retrieved the rig to find that the duck hadn't managed to get the bait from the rig this time. The only good thing about that last occurrence was that I think it must have scared the ducks a little bit, because they all swam away towards the far end of the lake. Unfortunately, I was pretty sure that they'd be back.

I re-casted all the rods and re-baited, but within half an hour the ducks returned and started diving on my baits again. Once again I tried all sorts of things to try to deter them. I tried firing boilies at them with a catapult, but that didn't work at all. They ate them as they fell through the water, and it seemed to encourage them all the more. Next I tried casting an empty spod at them, and retrieving it fast past them. This worked a little better and they retreated a short distance, but as soon as I put the rod down they came back.

My next idea was to catapult boilies a short distance away from my swim, hoping that they would move towards the sound of the boilies hitting the water, and away from me. They moved towards where I was now catapulting the boilies just as I had hoped, but as soon as I stopped, they went back and started to dive on my spots again.

I was tearing my hair out again in frustration, but all I could do was to ignore them and hope that they would eventually move away. Occasionally they would disappear for ten or fifteen minutes, but then they came back and started diving all over again. They must have picked up my hook-bait at least half a dozen times, but each time I just casted it back into position again. Then just after three o`clock the alarm sounded once again, but this time the bobbin rose to the rod butt and stayed there. I picked up the rod but immediately realised what was responsible, when a duck came to the surface and started to fly off with my hook-bait in it. The duck flew straight towards the bank, about thirty yards to my right, and as I tried to bring it towards me, my line caught in a bank-side bush. For a while it was stalemate. The duck couldn`t escape and I couldn`t bring it towards me, the duck just sat there shaking its head and thrashing the water. I had to unhook the duck to release it, so I went to my car to fetch my waders. I then waded along the deep margin until I could almost reach the duck. Unfortunately I wasn`t quite close enough, and the duck remained tantalisingly just out of reach. I pulled on the line and the duck started to come towards me at last, still thrashing the water as it did so. Suddenly the hook pulled, and the lead shot back and hit me hard on my face, just below my right eye.

So that`s the thanks I got for releasing the duck!

Strangely, while all of this was going on, all the other ducks were gathered around it, probably trying to make out what was happening to their friend.

The only good thing about this was that it seemed to deter the ducks from diving on my baits for a while. It didn`t stop them completely though, and about an hour or so later they were back, but at least they didn`t dive quite so much. While they were away, I wasn`t left in peace however, and during this time my hook-baits were disturbed another couple of times by coots.

I just couldn`t win!

The only good thing about the day so far, was the weather. Rather like the previous day, as time went by, it got warmer and warmer. If anything, it was even hotter than the previous day, and once again I was sat there in the warm sun in a tee-shirt and wearing sun glasses. It seemed unbelievable that the day had started with thick fog and frost.

I re-casted once again at six o`clock, and put out a sprinkling of bait, then I sat down to watch the water with a cup of tea. As I sat there, my remote sounded and the bobbin on my second rod lifted to the butt, and held there. This time there were no ducks or coots anywhere near, and to my delight, when I picked up the rod, I found myself connected to a fish at last. It didn`t seem particularly big, but I played it very carefully none-the-less. I placed the net in front of me and eased the fish to the surface, which was when I realised for the first time that it wasn`t a carp at all, but a large bream.

I was devastated.

The bream had picked up my tigernut snowman rig, which made it even harder to take. A bream on tigernuts just wasn`t fair. When I unhooked the bream, I noticed a lot of spawning tubercles on it, which really surprised me. The water was very cold indeed, and I would have thought that spawning was the last thing on their minds.

I`d just returned the bream when a car pulled up and out stepped Patrice. He was a good friend of mine that I used to fish with at Conty, and it was good to see him again. Anita had met Patrice too, when she came to Conty with me a couple of years before, and we both agreed that he was a lovely man and a very good friend. When I`d last seen Patrice, the previous October, he told me that he had hardly been fishing at all over the previous few months, but now he said that he had given up fishing completely, and had sold all of his tackle. He said that he had lost his motivation, and that he just didn`t want to go any more. He now preferred to spend his time playing darts. That was a great shame because he was a tremendous angler, and it was a sad loss to our sport. Patrice and I talked until just after dark, and then he wished me 'Bonne Peche' and drove off.

With the total lack of action that I had received from the carp, I was now starting to think that I had made a big error, and introduced too much bait. The water was very cold and it was only March after all, so the fish probably weren`t feeding very much. The only saving grace for me was the ducks and the coots which I had cursed so much, during the last couple of days. They were still occasionally diving on my spots, and picking up the boilies that I`d put there. My best chance was that the amount of bait out there would gradually get less and less, thanks to the bird-life. I decided that I wouldn`t introduce any more free bait, except just stringers, and perhaps I`d get a chance. It was a plan at least, and maybe I`d get lucky.

The next afternoon the ducks didn`t bother me at all for a change, but the coots went crazy. There were about a dozen of them, and they all decided that it was time for sex. This involved chasing each other all over the lake, thrashing the surface to a foam, and making more noise than I could ever have thought possible. Any carp present must have been frightened out of their lives, and I was sure that any slight chance that I may have had of catching a carp, was disappearing fast.

Why me?

I re-casted the rods just after seven o'clock that night. When I had casted my right-hand rod, the wind was blowing across me from right to left, and I had difficulty getting the rig where I wanted it, near to the far bank, because of the bow in the line. I managed to get it there, but I wasn't entirely happy with it. Just before dark the wind dropped, so I quickly retrieved the rig, re-tied the lead with pva tape, ready for a re-cast. Unfortunately the line caught around the butt ring on the cast, and I cracked off.

'Oh that's a shame' I said, or words to that effect.

It was now almost dark, so I knew that it would be virtually impossible to find the correct distance in the rapidly fading light. I couldn't clip up using the pole elastic marker that I'd put on the line, because I had lost a few feet of line when I cracked off, so I just put the rod back on the rest, and decided to fish with just three rods overnight. I would sort out the fourth rod in the morning.

Ten minutes later when I was sitting in my bivvy, changing the batteries in my head-torch, my remote sounded. I looked up and I saw that it was my second rod and that the indicator was tight to the rod.

I picked up the rod and started to play the fish, but before too long I realised that it wasn't a carp, and shortly afterwards I netted another bream. It had taken my tigernut bait, just like the bream that I'd caught the previous night.

Now although I do catch the occasional bream on tigernuts, they normally tend to deter bream to a certain extent, and I usually catch more carp than bream when I use them. This session however, I had caught two bream on tigernuts, and no carp, and what was even more surprising was that I hadn`t caught any bream at all on my boilies. I couldn`t help but feel that I wasn`t having the best of luck, and that I was destined not to catch any carp this session.

I decided not to re-cast the tigernuts on that rod, and I replaced it with an orange pop-up on a hinged stiff rig. It was not so much that I thought that I`d catch a carp on the pop-up, but more a case of trying to avoid the bream.

I woke on Thursday morning, and it was cold and overcast with a light north-easterly wind. When I re-casted the rods at just before half past ten, I repositioned the left-hand rod at about forty yards towards the bent tree. I remembered that I had caught three carp in March the previous year in that area, so I thought that it was worth a try. The water had been a lot warmer that year however, and to be honest, by this time I had already resigned myself to a blank. That didn`t mean that I had stopped trying of course, but I just didn`t think that it would happen. Once again I didn`t introduce any more bait. It wasn`t working, and obviously the fish weren`t feeding much, so I thought that adding more bait would only be counter-productive.

The coots seemed to be behaving themselves now. They are really stupid creatures, but even they had decided that it was far too cold to indulge in the sort of activity of the previous day.

Just after one o`clock that afternoon, much against my better judgement, I decided to put out a little bait. The area in which I was now fishing my left-hand rod hadn`t received any bait at all during the session, so I reasoned that it couldn't do any harm, especially if I didn't put out too much. In the end I just catapulted out twelve 16 mm. boilies and six 20 mm. spread in the general area of my left-hand rod. Just for good measure I also put out eight 20 mm. boilies with a throwing stick, along the far margin, where I was fishing with my right-hand rod. The ducks immediately swam over to investigate, but after diving just a couple of times, they moved off, so even the ducks weren't hungry.

That night was very cold and I was soon tucked up inside my sleeping bag to keep warm. I read a book for a while, but I hadn't heard a single bleep from the alarms or heard any activity from the carp, and eventually I dropped off to sleep, not expecting anything to happen at all. Just after half past eleven that night however, I was woken by my remote indicating a take. The blue light on my remote was flashing, which meant that it was my right-hand rod, the one that had been casted close to the far bank. It was the first action that I had received to that rod, and I hurried out of the bivvy, hoping that this could be my first carp of the session. I was fishing this rod with a tight line, and when I approached it, I noticed that the indicator had dropped down towards the floor, and my heart sank, thinking that it must be yet another bream. When I picked up the rod, sure enough it was a small fish, and I reeled in the 'bream' towards me. When I got the fish to the bank, I was in for a real surprise however, because it wasn't a bream at all, but a Tench. Now tench are a species that I have only ever caught in France during the summer months, in warm water conditions. Yet here I was in March, with the water so cold that I'd not been able to catch any carp, and I'd caught a tench.

Unbelievable!

After I'd returned the tench, I didn't bother to re-cast the rod, I just placed the rod on the rests and went back to bed, shaking my head in disbelief.

I reeled in the rods at about half past eight the following morning, and started a slow pack-up, before starting the journey back to England.

It had been a very disappointing trip overall, but I was due back in France in just over three weeks' time, when I would be fishing the main lake for the first time this year. I just hoped that in those three weeks the water would have warmed up enough to give me a chance of catching some of the big fish that lived in that lake.

CHAPTER THREE – THE MAIN LAKE

The journey down to Dover went without a hitch and I arrived at the port with more than an hour and a half to spare. The P & O chap said that I could go on the next ferry, which was boarding in ten minutes time which was excellent news, but then he discovered a problem. I had booked on the ferry which sailed at 2.20 a.m. but he couldn't find my booking. He thought that it was stranger that he couldn't find it, but luckily I had a print-out of the booking with me, so I gave that to him, and as soon as he looked at it he realised what the problem was.

'You have booked for 2.20 a.m. on 29th March' he said 'but today is 30th March!'

I had booked the wrong date!

I couldn't believe that I could have been so careless, but there it was in black and white. Fortunately I was still able to use my booking to travel, but there was a charge of £60 for changing the date. That was an expensive error on my part, and I'd make sure that I didn't make that mistake again.

With catching the earlier ferry, I arrived at the 'Main Lake' at Loeuilly at seven o'clock in the morning, just as it was getting light. I glanced at the temperature gauge on the car, which was showing nine degrees, and that wasn't too bad at all. In fact it was positively tropical compared to what I had to put up with at Contre just three weeks earlier, when it was -2 when I arrived. Although the temperature was higher this time, the water was still very cold, and there was a strong wind blowing, which didn't make it feel very pleasant at all. I knew from talking to a couple of my friends during the previous couple of weeks, that there hadn't been a single carp caught from the 'Main Lake' so far this year, so it certainly wasn't going to be easy.

There was no-body else there at all, so I had the choice of any swim on the lake that I wanted. I had a look around and I didn't see any signs of carp, but to be honest I didn't really expect to see any, because although the carp do tend to show themselves in this lake, that normally happens later in the year, but not in March. I decided to set-up about 100 yards along the west bank, in a swim that I had been successful in the previous year, and I set my bivvy up first to make myself comfortable. Once that was done I made myself a cup of coffee, and then had a quick lead around to see how much weed was out there. The last time that I'd fished in this swim it had been very weedy indeed and I'd had to spend quite a bit of time clearing some of the weed, just to make it fishable, but it wasn't like that this time however. There was a little light weed in places, but nothing that was likely to cause me any problems.

I soon found some good areas to fish to, and I decided to spod heavily onto one spot, but to bait with just boilies on the other three. After the initial baiting, I then intended to feed quite lightly on a little-and-often basis, and to see what happened.

By the time that I'd finished baiting-up, the wind had increased in strength quite a lot. It was gusty and kept changing direction, so it made it very difficult for me to cast my hook-baits accurately. I made one cast and the wind caught the line and blew the rig a couple of yards to the left. The next cast I tried to compensate for the wind by aiming a couple of yards to the right, hoping that the wind would drift it nicely into position. Of course this time the cast went straight as an arrow exactly where I had aimed it, so the rig ended up a couple of yards to the right.

Typical!

Eventually I managed to get all four hook-baits positioned as I wanted, and I sat down very relieved to have something to eat. I hadn`t been sat down long however when one of the delkims sounded.

'That was quick' I thought, but unfortunately it wasn`t a carp. It was just a strong gust of wind that had caused it, and over the next few minutes it happened several more times. I turned the sensitivity on my delkims down, but that didn`t solve the problem and in the end I had to turn the alarms onto the minus settings, and that did the trick.

Nothing much happened that afternoon and I started to re-cast the rods at about six o`clock that evening, ready for the night ahead. I was using pop-up`s on two rods (one white and one orange, but both with the same flavours as my free-bait), one with a snowman, and on the last rod I had a double bottom-bait, so I was trying to cover as many options as I could. I just didn`t know what would work in these conditions, so it seemed like a sensible idea.

When I was half-way through re-casting the rods, I heard a shout of 'Hello', and when I turned around I saw my good friend Clément and his girl-friend Camille. I hadn`t seen Clément for some time because he`d been working in Paris. He is a fireman, and he had been training with the Paris fire-fighters, which were the elite fire-fighters of the whole of France. He told me that he had passed his training a couple of months earlier, so now he was officially part of the Paris fire-fighters brigade.

Quite an achievement.

The three of us talked for a while, and then Clément and Camille went to have their evening meal, but Clément said that he`d return later that night with a couple of beers.

The night was quite mild but the wind, which was a light south-westerly at first, changed to a more southerly direction, and it became much stronger as time went by. By two or three o'clock on Tuesday morning the wind was very strong indeed, and it was really howling down the lake. Although I was quite tired after the journey, I was unable to sleep in those conditions, and I was worried that the bivvy and everything in it were literally going to be blown away. Branches and other various objects were continually being sent crashing into the bivvy, and with the noise of the wind it really was quite frightening. Fortunately everything held firm, but it definitely wasn't one of the most pleasant nights that I'd spent on the bank.

What's that old saying?

'March comes in like a lamb and leaves like a lion'.

Well the lions certainly roared that night.

When I woke at first light on Tuesday morning I wasn't at all surprised that I hadn't caught anything during that horrendous night, but I was just glad to have survived it. When the storm had been at its peak in the early hours, I had visions of my session ending right there, with my bivvy blown into the lake.

When I emerged from my bivvy to check on the rods, they were all still in position, which was a relief, but the landing nets were a different matter. I normally use two nets and I had propped them up on bank-sticks off of the floor, to keep them away from any rats that might be around, and both of them had been blown off of the rests. One of the nets was just a few yards along the bank, but the other had actually been blown into the lake. I could just see the very end of the handle sticking up out of the water, and fortunately I was able to retrieve it.

The wind was not quite as bad as it had been, but it was still very strong, so I decided not to re-cast the rods. There was very little chance of getting the rigs where I wanted them in these conditions, so I thought that I might as well leave them where they were for the time being. I`d been reasonably happy with the casts that I`d made the previous night, but I just hoped that there was still bait on the rigs. There are some crayfish present in this lake, which have caused me problems in the past, but hopefully the cold water conditions that had so far helped to prevent me from catching any carp, would mean that the crayfish weren`t so active. I hoped that the wind would subside a little that evening, and I would then be able to change the hook-baits and re-cast them.

At half past twelve I put out just twenty 16mm. boilies and eight twenty mm. around each rod, and I was pleased that I was able to get the baits out there quite accurately in the strong wind. I am not the best with a throwing-stick by any means, and I normally prefer to use a catapult where possible, because I think that it`s far more accurate. In that wind however, I would never have been able to reach the distance to my spots with a catapult, so I used a throwing-stick instead, and despite my lack of practice, the results were very satisfying.

At least something was going right.

Although the wind was not quite as bad as before, there were gusts from time to time that were very strong indeed, and which caused the delkims to bleep, despite the sensitivity being turned right down. The gusts of wind were so strong that it caused the rod-tips to bend and shake, which is what was causing these false bleeps. At about half past three that afternoon I heard three or four bleeps coming from one of my delkims yet again, but when I looked, I saw the indicator drop a few inches, and then rise again to the rod and hold there.

'That`s not the wind.' I said to myself, and I hurried towards it. When I picked up the rod I could feel a heavy weight on the end of the line, but it wasn`t doing much. I bent the rod into it and felt the fish kick as it moved slightly towards me, and my heart soared as I realised that I`d hooked a carp at last. The fish didn`t make any long or fast runs, it just plodded around slowly as I gradually worked it back towards me, and I realised that it could be a very big fish. With less weed in the lake than normal, I didn`t encounter any problems, and I soon caught sight of the fish for the first time, as I brought it to the surface in front of me. It was a mirror, and a good one at that, and fortunately it went into the net at the first attempt. I staked the net with a bank-stick to make it safe, and then I punched the air with delight.

I then went into the bivvy to get my phone, and I rang Benoit. I told him about the fish and asked him if he was coming to the lake that evening. Unfortunately he said that he couldn`t get there that day, but that he`d be along to see me on Friday evening.

'No problem' I replied, 'I`ll do some self-takes.'

I then had another idea and rang Clément. I asked if he was working, and he told me that he had the day off and was at home. He said that he had to go to the dentist`s first, but that he`d come to help with the photos after that.

'That`s a bit of luck.' I thought.

I never mind doing self-takes, but with a big fish, it`s always much easier with a friend to help. I knew that Clément was very good with a camera, so I had no worries about letting him take the photos for me.

I carried the fish to the mat and had a good look at it. It was a beautiful fish which I guessed was probably just under forty pounds, but it was a young fish with a big frame and it looked as though it would grow a lot bigger in the not too distant future. I put it into the sling, which I`d already zeroed, and hoisted it onto the scales. The needle swung round the dial on the scales and then flickered around just short of 36½ pounds, so I settled on a weight of 36 lbs.6 oz.

I put the fish into a sack which I carefully placed in the deep margin, and I was pleased to see the fish move away from the bank in the sack, tightening the cord as it went. It then settled on the lake-bed and sat there quite happily. I would keep checking on the fish from time to time until Clément arrived, but I knew that it would be fine.

I then re-casted both of my left-hand rods and sticked out a few more boilies around them. I had caught the fish on my second rod, on a spot that had been successful for me the last time that I`d fished in this swim, and fortunately I managed to get it back out there perfectly first time. The other rod was a little more difficult, and it took me three attempts before I was happy with it. I then went back to my bivvy to make myself a well-deserved cup of tea.

Clément arrived at about half past six with his girl-friend Camille and Timothée, who was another friend of ours. The sun had come out and was at a difficult angle for the photos, but as usual, Clément did a superb job with the camera.

Thanks mate!

They all left about an hour later, but Clément promised to return on Thursday afternoon to fish with me in the 'Big Back Lake'. It would be good to have some company while I was fishing for a change and I just hoped that we could catch a couple of carp to make it even better.

I had intended to re-cast my other two rods ready for the night, but by half past seven, instead of easing, the wind seemed to be getting worse. There was still more than an hour until it got dark, so I hoped that the wind would drop enough to allow me to re-cast, but if not, I'd leave those two baits in position for another night. There was a slight lull about twenty minutes later which allowed me to re-cast my third rod, but that lull didn't last long, so the fourth rod stayed where it was.

Just after eight o'clock Vincent came to see me, and he was just getting out of his car when I heard one of my delkims again. It was my left-hand rod this time, and I found myself connected to another carp. It didn't feel quite as big as the last one and a few minutes later Vincent was able to lift the net around it. It was another mirror of 26 lbs.10 oz. and Vincent took the photos.

The carp had taken an orange pop-up, the same as the last one, so I re-casted the rod with another orange pop-up. It seemed to be working so I saw no reason to change. I have an assortment of different coloured pop-ups, but I make them all with the same flavours and attractors as the free-baits, and they do seem to work very well. Surprisingly, despite the severe cross-wind, the cast hit the spot perfectly first time, much to my relief. I still didn't re-cast my fourth rod though. It was starting to get dark by now and I decided to leave it and try to re-cast it in the morning instead, when hopefully the wind would have dropped and the cast would be easier.

Vincent left shortly after dark and I was soon tucked up inside my sleeping bag and fast asleep. I didn't stay there all night however, because at about four o'clock the next morning I was woken by a screaming delkim. I was soon out of the bivvy to investigate, but unfortunately the excitement didn't last long, and I soon landed a big slimey bream – not quite what I wanted in the middle of the night. The bream had taken a snowman bait on my third rod, but I didn't bother to re-cast it, and instead I just put the rod back on the rests and went back to bed.

The next day was a lot cooler with broken cloud, but the wind had dropped at last, and was now just a light to moderate north-easterly, so I was able to recast the two rods on my right. I put a little more bait around all the spots and then sat down to watch the water. I sat there all morning watching, but I didn't see any signs of fish at all, but my two fish so far had been caught in the afternoon and evening, so I hoped that perhaps I'd get another chance later that day.

Around mid-day I decided to re-cast my second rod. This was the rod on which I'd caught the 36 the previous day, and I'd not had any action to that rod since then. I retrieved the rig and re-sharpened the hook, and then I tied on a new pop-up and balanced it with putty, ready to re-cast. Just as I was about to make the cast, the wind began to gust strongly from left to right, so rather than try to cast in such a severe cross-wind, I decided to wait. I propped the rod up against the bivvy and secured it with the little Velcro fasteners that are fixed to my overwrap, and then I sat down to wait for the wind to drop again. I had been sat there for perhaps two or three minutes when one of my delkims let out a series of bleeps. It was my left-hand rod, the one that I'd caught a mirror on the previous evening, when Vincent was with me. The indicator was tight to the rod and the line was out of the clip when I reached the rod, which I picked up quickly and felt a heavy resistance on the end of the line. I carefully started to ease it towards me, but the fish had other ideas. I managed to slowly gain five or six yards of line, but then the fish powered away from me taking fifteen or twenty yards of line back, and I had to start all over again. It was a very

34

powerful fish, but I knew that the weed wasn`t too bad and that there weren`t many bad snags, so as long as I took my time and the hook held, then I should be alright. It took more than twenty minutes, but finally I saw the fish on the surface, just ten yards in front of me. It was a big mirror which looked as if it might go forty, and I could see the pop-up hanging from its mouth as I drew it towards me. I was praying that the hook would hold as I drew it over the net-cord and lifted. It went into the net at the first attempt and I felt very relieved and elated all at the same time, but I almost managed to botch it all up even then. As I pulled the landing net towards me, the pole snapped where it joined the spreader block. I quickly bent down and grabbed the net, with the fish still inside, and secured it to the bank with a bank-stick, then breathed another huge sigh of relief. This had happened to me once before when my landing net pole had snapped in the same place, when I netted a big grass carp the previous year. I had mended the pole and had thought that it was alright, but perhaps now was the time for me to buy a new one. The price of a landing net pole had nearly cost me a big fish, and I didn`t want to make that mistake again. Fortunately I always carry two nets with me when I`m fishing, so I`d be able to use the other one for the rest of the session.

I knew that Benoit and Vincent were working, so that they wouldn`t be able to help me with the photos, and I was pretty sure that Clément was working too, but I rang him just to make sure. When I rang it went straight through to answer phone, so I assumed that he was working and I decided to take the photos myself.

I took my time getting everything ready to weigh the fish, and then I set up the camera on its tripod. I use an air release system to do my self-takes, and once the camera is set up properly, all I have to do is kneel in position and press my knee on the rubber bulb, and the camera shutter is operated. I knelt in position first and took a couple of test shots, which seemed perfect, and then I went to get the fish.

As soon as I lifted it out of the water in the net, and started to carry it towards the mat, I realised that it was bigger than I had thought. It was definitely over 40, but how big was it?

I opened the net on the mat, and saw the carp properly for the first time, and it looked enormous. The hook-hold was perfect in the middle of the bottom lip, and I unhooked it and the carefully placed it into the sling, which I`d already zeroed. I hoisted it onto the scales on my weighing tripod and watched in disbelief as the needle on the dial span straight past 40 and fifty, before it dropped back and flickered around fifty before stopping just below. I looked carefully and finally settled on a weight of 49 lbs.14 oz. Another 2 oz. to make it 50 would have been nice, but I wasn`t bothered about that at all, because it was such a magnificent fish.

I took the sling off of the scales and placed the fish back on the mat where I put plenty of water on it, before starting to take the photos. As I lifted the big fish up for the camera, it behaved superbly, and I managed to take seven or eight good shots of the fish, before I was forced to put it down, gasping for breath. The second side of the fish wasn`t quite so easy, because I was very tired, and I struggled to lift the fish high enough, but I finally did manage to get three shots of that side, although they weren`t perfect.

I`m used to doing self-takes, but with a fish of that size it would have been so much easier with a friend or two to help me. I didn`t want to keep the fish out of the water for too long, so I put it back into the sling and carried it to the margin. I let it go and watched in wonder as the great beast swam slowly away. It would have been nice to get a few more good photos, but seeing it swim away, none the worse for its ordeal, was far more important.

After I'd released the fish, I re-casted that rod, and also the second rod which was still propped up against the bivvy where I had left it. I then sticked out a few more boilies and then returned to my bivvy to text a few mates, to let them know the good news. I was on a massive high, and it would take me a long time to come down.

About four o'clock that afternoon Eddie came to see me. I had met Eddie the previous year when we fished together on the Mystery Lake at Contre. We had got on really well, but I hadn't seen him since. Somehow he had heard about my big fish, and he had come to the lake to congratulate me. I showed him the photos and he said that it was a superb fish and shook my hand. He then told me about 'The Big Lake' at Conty. He had been fishing at 'The Big Lake' on and off for about two years, and he told me that it contained several carp that were even bigger than the one that I'd just caught. Now I'd fished at Conty about three years before, but only on the first and second lakes there. I knew that 'The Big Lake' contained the biggest fish, but it was strictly private, so I had never fished there. Eddie however, said that he could get me a guest ticket to fish there if I wanted.

I couldn't believe my ears. I definitely wanted to fish there, and I thanked him for his generosity, but I told him that I couldn't fish there for some time, because I already had several trips planned. My next trip was back to Loeuilly for the Enduro, and then in mid-May Anita and I were going on holiday, touring all over France in our caravan for two months, and we wouldn't return to England until mid-July. That was a holiday however, not a fishing trip, so I wouldn't be taking any tackle with me (well not unless I could sneak a small rod in without Anita knowing). I thanked Eddie again for the offer of a guest ticket, and asked if I could go sometime in the future, to which he replied –

'No problem, just tell me when you want to go and I'll try to arrange it for you.'

What a good friend!

Eddie then showed me a few photos of some of the carp from 'The Big Lake' that he and a friend of his had caught there, and they looked tremendous. That really got me wanting to fish there but I knew that it would be quite some time until I could.

Nothing of note happened during the rest of the afternoon, and I re-casted three of the rods at about half-past seven that evening, ready for the night. I left my right-hand rod in position. I had casted it out that morning with a snowman rig on and I didn't see any point in changing it. That was the only rod that hadn't produced any fish, although the one fished to the spodded area had only produced one bream, so that wasn't much better. I remembered the last time that I'd spodded on this lake, in September of the previous year, and the spodded area hadn't produced any carp then either, so I decided that perhaps I'd do better using a boilies-only approach on all rods, when I came here the next time.

This trip was for seven days and I'd decided to split it between the Main Lake and The Big Back Lake, so I was going to move in the morning, and spend the last four days on the other lake. I'd had a wonderful result on the Main Lake, but nothing I did there could possibly top that, so I was happy to move and try a new challenge.

Friday was a bank holiday (Good Friday) as it was Easter-time. So by moving on Thursday morning I should have a choice of swims, and be all set up before any-one else arrived. No-one else had fished either lake during the three days that I had been there so far, and these lakes never get very busy, but I expected that there would probably be a few people that would decide to fish over the holiday week-end. It`s not that I`m unsociable, but I`d been lucky having these lakes to myself, and I liked it that way.

It was dark just before nine o`clock that night and I was soon tucked up nice and warm in my sleeping bag. The wind had dropped a lot, and it was relatively calm for the first time since I`d been there. Perhaps my last night on this lake would bring me another fish, but I really didn`t mind because I was quite happy with what I`d caught.

I woke at dawn and was disappointed to hear a pitta-patter noise on the bivvy roof –

It was raining!

Apart from a short five minute spell early in the week, this was the first rain since I`d arrived, so I felt a little unlucky that it coincided with the morning that I intended to move to a different lake. I hate packing-up and setting-up in the rain. I don`t mind it so much once the bivvy is up, but if everything gets wet while I`m setting up, it`s often very difficult to get it all dry again. Unless the rain stopped soon however, I would have to move in the rain.

I hadn`t heard a single bleep from my delkims during the night, but that wasn`t unexpected. I`d caught all three of my carp during daylight hours, and just one bream during the night, which allowed me to get a good nights sleep, so that suited me fine.

I ate some breakfast and drank a cup of coffee, hoping that the rain would stop, but no such luck and at eleven o`clock that morning I took the rods out and started the soggy move to the other lake.

CHAPTER FOUR – THE BIG BACK LAKE

It was still raining when I arrived at the Big Back Lake, and I quickly settled on a swim two-thirds of the way along the far bank, where I had fished the previous year. The first thing for me to do was to set up the bivvy, so that I could keep everything dry. I had just laid out the ground-sheet on the floor when Vincent arrived, and with his help the bivvy was soon in place. I always struggle to pull the overwrap over the bivvy by myself, but with one of us on either side, it was fitted in no time at all. Vincent had brought his bait-boat with him, which is fitted with an echo sounder, because he wanted to use it to have a look at the features on the lake-bed, and to get an idea of the depths of the water. He thought that this information might help us if we drew a swim on this lake in the Enduro, which we were due to fish just three weeks later. Unfortunately he had forgotten to bring a battery cable with him, and his bait-boat wouldn`t work without it, so that was the end of that idea. He stayed for half an hour or so, and then he said that he had to go to work, so he wished me 'Bonne Pêche', and went on his way. Of course, now that I had set up, it stopped raining.

Now why couldn`t that have happened a couple of hours earlier?

I decided not to use a marker rod, and just used a lead on my normal rods to find the spots to fish. I already knew the depths in the various parts of the swim, having fished there before, so it was a simple matter of feeling the lead along the lake-bed, and when I found a spot that felt good, I put the line in the clip. One more cast to make sure, then I marked the line with pole elastic, and that was that. I was only using two rods because there wasn`t much room in the swim, so it didn`t take long.

40

The next job was to bait up, and I decided to use just boilies of two different sizes, plus a few tigernuts. To do this I casted a small lead out into the swim, on my rod which was already clipped-up, and then I catapulted the boilies into the rings made by the cast.

Easy!

Once the baiting was done, I positioned a pop-up on each spot, and then I made myself something to eat and a nice cup of tea. It was mid-afternoon by this time and I didn't realise how hungry I was until I started eating, but it was a long time since breakfast and I soon realised that I was famished.

Clément arrived at about half past four and he told me that he wouldn't be fishing with me in the Back Lake after all. He had his cousin with him who didn't have the necessary permits to fish the Back Lake, so they would be fishing the Main Lake instead. I think that my capture of the big mirror from the Main Lake the previous day may have helped him make that decision. We shared a beer, and I told him where I had positioned my hook-baits on the Main Lake, and Clément said that he would try to position his baits in the same places.

During the afternoon and early evening, my delkims sounded on four occasions, but unfortunate three times this was caused by coots picking up the hook-bait, and the fourth by a duck.

Don't you just love bird-life!

I re-casted for the night at about seven o'clock, with tigernuts on one rod and an orange pop-up on the other. I just had to have an orange pop-up on one rod after I'd caught the big mirror on one, the day before.

Clément came back to see me a couple of hours after dark, and this time Camille was with him. Over the next hour or so we drank a couple of beers and put the world to rights. It was quite a mild night and the wind had dropped completely, so it was quite pleasant as we stood there talking. Clément told me that he'd managed to find the spots that I'd fished on the Main Lake, and that both of his hook-baits were on gravel.

'That's not where I was fishing I'm afraid Clément' I told him. 'I was fishing on silt, and there was no gravel anywhere near.'

He was quite disappointed when I told him this, but I said that although he wasn't fishing on the same spots that I had done, that didn't mean that there was anything wrong with where he was fishing, and I hoped that he'd be able to tell me that he'd caught a large carp when I saw him the next day.

The night passed without a single bleep from my delkims, but I wasn't too dispirited because I often find that the second day is better than the first, especially if I've introduced a reasonable amount of bait, so there was still plenty of time.

I re-casted both rods at mid-day, and freshened up the spots with just a handful of boilies and a few tigernuts. The coots were still diving over my spots, so I knew that there was still some bait out there, and I didn't need to add too much more.

The two positions that I had been fishing were both in open water, both at between 35 and 40 yards range, and because I hadn't heard a bleep from my alarms during the night, not even a liner, I decided to fish with one rod in the margin that night. I didn't fancy the left margin, but the right-hand margin seemed perfect. I found a spot about five yards from the bank, where the lake-bed felt clear and fairly firm, as if something had fed there recently. It seemed perfect and I baited there lightly with a mixture of hemp, chopped boilies, chopped tigernuts, pellets and a handful of sweetcorn. I also trailed some of the same all along the margin to my right, although more sparsely. My plan was that any fish feeding along the margin would follow the trail of bait, and end up on my baited spot, where my hook-bait would be waiting for them. I didn`t fish the margin spot at this point, but left it with no lines anywhere near, and continued to fish my other two spots.

At about one o`clock that afternoon my left-hand hook-bait was disturbed by one of the dreaded coots yet again. I had been using a snowman rig wrapped in boilie-paste on that rod, and I couldn`t be bothered to dry it all off, and wrap it in paste again, especially if the coots were going to disturb it on a regular basis, so I just tied a pop-up onto a hinged stiff rig, and casted that out instead. I hoped that if the coots did pick up that rig, then it should re-set itself, and I wouldn`t have to continually keep re-casting.

I re-casted my rods for the night just after five o`clock, and this time I positioned a hook-bait in the right-hand margin. Because it seemed so clear, I decided to use my favourite method of a light running lead on a slack fluorocarbon main-line. Normally this lake is very weedy and I would never dare to fish in that way here, but the weed-growth was far less than normal this year, so I thought that it was worth a try.

I had just positioned my second rod when Clément and Camille arrived, and we were joined shortly afterwards by Benoit, so we all had a beer together once again. It sounds as though we do nothing but drink, but in actual fact we only drank one beer each, and they were only small bottles at that. I think they hold about a third of a pint, so we didn`t drink much, but it was very enjoyable all the same.

Unfortunately, just like me, Clément hadn`t managed to catch anything the previous night. That would be the last time that he would be able to fish for a while because he had to return to Paris to work, but at least I had another three nights in which to open my account on this lake.

The night was mild without a breath of wind and with occasional showers, which were reasonably good conditions, but although I watched the water carefully until dark, I didn`t see any signs of carp at all, and my alarms stayed silent. It remained that way during the first part of the night, so it came as a complete surprise when my left-hand delkim sounded just after half past ten. As I reached the rod I saw that the indicator had dropped right back to the ground, but to my dismay, when I picked up the rod, I found nothing on the other end of the line, and I reeled in the rig. The lead had discharged on the take, just as I`d hoped it would, but I suspected that the culprit was probably a bream.

I had another rig tied up ready with the bait on the hair, so I simply clipped my line back up to the mark, tied on the new rig and sent it back out there. It was almost a full moon. Although you would never have known it due to the cloud cover, and it was very dark. Despite this however, I could still make out the tall tree on the far bank against the skyline, which gave me the direction of the cast, and it went back perfectly.

I awoke at first light to a cold morning, with a fresh north-westerly wind. Since the occurrence on my left-hand rod at half past ten the previous evening, I hadn`t heard a single bleep from my alarms all night, and it certainly didn`t look very promising now, so I did the only sensible thing –

I turned over and went back to sleep.

When I finally got out of bed about an hour or so later, the conditions were no better. If anything it was worse because

44

the wind was stronger which made it feel even colder, and it was raining heavily. I made myself some breakfast and a cup of coffee, and decided to make a couple of changes. I replaced my right-hand hook-bait back onto its original position. I had fished that one in the margin overnight, but that hadn't produced anything, and the ducks were taking an unhealthy interest in the marginal spot, which wasn't helping at all. I kept chasing them away, but as soon as I returned to the bivvy, they were back again. My original spot for that rod had been left baited but unfished since the previous evening, so I hoped that it might now produce something. I used a snowman rig on that rod wrapped in boilies paste and for a change on my left-hand rod I used a single grain of yellow plastic sweetcorn, which I had soaked in thaumatin, on one of my little looped stiff rigs. I hoped that this would surely provoke some interest from something, if only from a bream.

I topped up both areas with just a sprinkling of boilies, and then I went back to my bivvy to shelter from the rain. It remained showery all day, but as time went by it became even colder. Fortunately by evening the rain had stopped, but it was so cold that I sat there wearing two fleeces, a thick coat and a woolly hat, and I still didn't feel warm. The wind was now from a northerly direction and it had a real bite to it. Yet again I hadn't heard a sound from my delkims, and even the coots and the ducks had stopped diving on my baits.

'If even the bird-life doesn't want to eat my baits, then what chance is there of a fish?' I thought.

Benoit dropped by for a short visit to check that I was ok and to bring me some milk, because I had drunk so much coffee that I'd used it all. He stood there shivering, and then he wished me good luck, told me to call him if I needed any help with some photos, then he hurried back to his warm home.

I re-casted the rods at six o`clock that evening, both with balanced baits and srtingers, and then I made myself something warm to eat. That made me feel a lot better, but it certainly wasn`t getting any warmer, and before long I was tucked up inside my sleeping bag.

The night was very cold and the surface of the lake was flat calm. Once again I didn`t hear a single bleep from the alarms and when I woke in the morning there was a heavy frost. Within a couple of hours of daybreak however, everything looked better. The sun was shining down out of a cloudless blue sky, and my confidence soared. Perhaps there was a chance of me catching a carp here before I left the next morning, after all.

I decided however, that I was going to have to find some new positions to fish. Fishing over beds of bait had not worked at all, so I thought that I`d try singles, fished away from those baited areas. I also decided to use an extra rod. I used three different coloured pop-ups, two on 360 rigs and the third on a hinged stiff rig, and I didn`t put any bait around them at all. I was just hoping that a carp would swim through one of these areas and decide to dip down and pick up one of these pop-ups. I didn`t know if it would work or not, but it was worth a try.

Unfortunately by mid-afternoon there were several clouds obscuring the sun, a bitter north-east wind had sprung up and it had become surprisingly cold. I realised that the water temperature wasn`t going to rise much any time soon, and my chances of catching a carp were receding fast. I made myself something to eat. It was sweet and sour chicken with rice, which was delicious, but it didn`t make me feel any more optimistic about my chances.

That night was once again very cold, with a clear sky and not a breath of wind. I heard a couple of bleeps from my right-hand rod just after dark, which was probably caused by a coot, but that was it, and when I woke in the morning there was thick fog and another heavy frost. Fortunately the sun soon broke through the fog, so at least I was able to pack up in the dry.

When I looked back on the trip, it was hard to believe how different the two lakes were. I'd caught three carp in three days on the Main Lake to almost fifty pounds, which was incredible, but then four days on the Back Lake with no carp and not even a bream was terribly disappointing. My next trip to France would be in just over two weeks time, when I was going to fish in the Enduro with Vincent, and I must admit that I wasn't very optimistic about that. With all those people on the bank and all that noise, I wasn't expecting much to be caught, but I would spend four days on the middle lake at Contre afterwards, and hopefully that would make up for it.

CHAPTER FIVE – THE ENDURO

In the couple of weeks before the Enduro, I tried to make sure that I had everything ready. Vincent would be using my rigs, so I tied up a few more, just to make sure that there were enough for both of us. I was finishing the last of the rigs on the Sunday afternoon before I was due to go back to France. I was making a 360 rig and I tied the hook-link to the ring swivel, but as I pulled hard to tighten the knot, it slipped and I found myself staring at the middle finger of my left hand, which had a size six long-shank curved hook deeply imbedded into it.

Ooopst!

Now I have managed to get a hook stuck into my hand once before. It was when I was at Woodland Waters a couple of years ago and In that case I had managed to remove it myself. It took me a little time, and there was a great deal of pain and blood involved, but I had got the hook out. This was a different thing altogether however, and it soon became apparent that I was going to need some help, so off I went to A&E. When I got to the hospital they had a look at it and then sent me to have it x-rayed. Now I expected the nurses to be quite comforting, but the first nurse took a look and said that looks awful, and turned away. Then the nurse who was taking the x-rays said that it made her feel weak at the knees, so they certainly weren`t making me feel much better. About an hour or so later the results were back which showed that not only was the hook embedded deep into my finger, but it had also penetrated the bone. The doctor said that they would first pull the hook out of the bone, and then they would cut the hook-shank and push it through my finger and out of the side. They couldn`t pull the hook out the way that it had gone in because of the barb, so pushing it right through was the best way to proceed. Fortunately they would give me an injection so that I wouldn`t feel too much pain. Now that sounded pretty gruesome, but the doctor seemed to know what he was doing.

By now my finger had swollen to about twice its normal size, and I was in quite a lot of pain, so you can imagine what it was like when the doctor stuck the needle in my finger. The pain was excruciating and I nearly leapt off the bed! He injected my finger in two places and fortunately that soon made it completely numb and I wasn`t in any more pain. The doctor took quite a long time, but eventually he was able to remove the hook and I thanked him profusely. One good thing was that because it was a brand new hook, straight out of the packet, the doctor said that there wouldn`t be any need for an anti-biotic, so he applied a bandage and sent me on my way.

All this was just a few days before the Enduro, so it wasn`t quite the perfect preparation. The next day it was still very sore and extremely swollen, so I just hoped that It would soon improve and that it wouldn`t restrict my fishing too much.

I arrived at Loeuilly at about seven o`clock in the morning, to find the sun shining from a clear blue sky and I realised that it was going to be a hot day. I parked the car, and had a walk around the three lakes that were to be used for the Enduro. I decided that because of all the disturbance that would be created, I would prefer to draw a swim at either end of one of the lakes, rather than a middle swim. My thinking was that if we stayed quiet, the carp would move away from the noise and into our swim, which seemed like a plan. After walking around the lakes a couple of times, I decided that the swims I would really like were number 8 on the big Back Lake, number 6 on the small Back Lake and

Number 1 on the Main Lake. Now all we had to do was to draw one of them.

Vincent arrived at ten o'clock, an hour and a half before the draw, and I told him about my swim preference, and he said that as I knew the lake far better than he did, that he was happy to do whatever I thought was best.

The draw would decide the order in which the swims were chosen, so for example, the person drawing number one would choose their swim first, number two would choose next, and so on. Eleven thirty finally arrived and the draw began. I let Vincent draw the number out of the bag and he got number 8. There were seventeen teams in total, so it could have been a lot worse, but it could also have been a lot better. It meant that we had eighth choice of swim and there were seven teams to choose before us. Amazingly almost all of the those seven teams chose to fish on the main lake and when it came to our choice, my preferred two swims, number eight and number six, were both still available.

'Take number eight' I said, to which Vincent replied 'Are you sure Steve?'

'Definitely, it's the one I've wanted all along' I said.

So that was it. We would be spending the next four days in swim number 8 on the Big Back Lake, and I couldn't have been happier.

It was now time to put our plan into action. What we decided to do was to keep well back from the water's edge, staying very quiet and not cast in until the match was a few hours old. By doing this and leaving the swim without any lines in the water, we hoped that the carp would move away from the disturbance caused by the other anglers and into our swim. It was very hot and sunny that afternoon so we thought that we wouldn't be missing much by not fishing for the first few hours of the match because we didn`t think that the carp would be feeding in those conditions anyway.

It didn`t take long for us to realise that our plan wasn`t working, because within ten minutes of the start of the match, a grass carp of over thirty pounds was caught in the Main lake. The successful angler had spodded a large bed of bait out into his swim, causing a lot of disturbance, and had then caught a fish almost straight away.

So much for our idea of light baiting and a stealthy approach being the way to go.

We consoled ourselves by thinking that it was only one fish and there was plenty of time left, but then two carp were hooked at the opposite end of our lake. Both of those carp were lost due to hook-pulls, but that wasn`t much consolation, because the carp didn`t seem to be at our end of the lake at all.

Nothing happened for us during the night, but early the next morning two carp were caught in our lake. They were both caught at the opposite end of the lake and our swim looked totally lifeless. There was also a carp caught in the Main Lake which was a magnificent mirror of over fifty pounds.

At about ten o`clock that morning the stewards arrived with coffee, croissants and 'pain et chocolat' for us all.

Trés bien!

Although it was a completion, I was amazed how friendly everyone was. Whenever we saw another angler, they always shook hands and wished us luck, and everyone seemed pleased whenever a carp was caught.

A lovely atmosphere.

I tryed many different things to try to induce a bite but nothing seemed to work. I soaked the boilies in the water that I had used to boil the hemp and then added hemp oil. The boilies gave off a lovely slick from the oil as I catapulted them into the swim which looked very attractive. I then fished with solid pva bags of boilie crumb and hemp oil, and I was sure that if there were any carp in the area, that these methods must provoke some interest, but that was the problem –

There didn't appear to be any carp there.

Nothing further was caught during the night but once again there was a fish caught at the opposite end of our lake in the morning, and it was a fantastic fish, a mirror of fifty-one pounds and fourteen ounces.

I was absolutely stunned by that capture because I had no idea that there were fish of that size in this lake. I knew that there were big fish in the Main Lake because I had caught one of almost fifty pounds myself, the previous month. Benoit and Clément had told me about a huge mirror of about mid-fifties that they called 'Dominator', which lived in the Small Back Lake, but I hadn't thought that there was anything over forty pounds in the Big Back Lake. This capture meant that there were now huge fish in all three lakes, so perhaps I should spend more time here in the future. I had a season ticket, so I could fish there whenever I wanted, but in the past I had neglected these smaller lakes and concentrated on the Main Lake.

Perhaps that was a mistake.

On Saturday afternoon we decided to introduce a lot of bait. We had nothing to lose, and we just hoped that it might encourage a few fish to feed. I must admit that I doubted if it would work, because I thought that the problem was that there weren't any carp in our swim, but it was worth a try. I had resigned myself to a blank by now, so it came as a big surprise when I was woken by my remote at about two o'clock on Sunday morning. Vincent was using two of my delkims and when I saw the green light on the remote was flashing, I realised that it was one of Vincent's rods, so I shouted his name to let him know, but there was no reply. I walked towards his rods and saw that line was being taken off the spool, so I shouted Vincent again, but once more there was no reply.

'OK I'll do it then' I said to myself, and I picked up the rod.

What I didn't realise, was that Vincent was fishing with the clutch on his reels set very slack indeed, so when I tried to make contact with the fish, line just poured off the reel and I almost fell over backwards. Fortunately I soon realised what the problem was, so I tightened the clutch and soon had the fish in front of me. It went into the net quite easily, but when I shone my torch into the net the sight that greeted me wasn't what I wanted to see at all. I knew that it wasn't a large carp, but it wasn't a carp at all, it was a big bream. Well I'd landed the fish for him, but I wasn't about to get covered in bream slime too.

'Vincent can deal with it himself' I thought so I banged on his bivvy roof to wake him, and called his name again, but unbelievably there was still no reply. As a last resort, I unzipped his bivvy door and shone my torch on his head, and finally he stirred. I told him that there was a fish in his net, and he hurried to have a look, but wasn't impressed when he discovered that it was a bream. I laughed and left him to deal with the slimy pest. Vincent had the last laugh though, when I caught a bream myself just after dawn.

The Enduro finished at eleven o'clock that morning and after packing all of our tackle into the cars, we went to the presentation. The Mayor gave a speech and then four large trophies were presented, one for each of the first three teams, and one for the largest fish. There was just one last trophy to present and that was a three foot long wooden spoon. There were seven teams that had failed to catch, and they put seven pieces of paper into a bag. On these were written the numbers one to seven and each team that had failed to catch would draw one out of the bag. The team that drew number seven would win the wooden spoon. Of course no-one wanted to win the wooden spoon and Vincent told me to draw for our team. I put my hand in the bag and drew out a paper, and was very relieved to see a number 2 written on it. The unlucky winners were then made to drink whiskey out of the wooden spoon, while we all clapped and cheered. When the formalities were over, there was a meal for all of us including champagne, and a good time was had by all.

CHAPTER SIX – THE MIDDLE LAKE

After leaving Loeuilly, I drove to Contre, where I arrived at about one o`clock in the afternoon. I was looking forward to fishing the Middle lake for the first time this year, and I knew exactly where I wanted to fish. Now I don`t normally chose a swim before I arrive at any venue, but the Middle Lake was different. The swim was on the east bank of the lake, tucked away on the edge of a forest. It was the weediest part of the lake, and there were always some fish there, but no-one else seemed to fish the swim. Most of the French anglers normally fished from the middle of the lake, where it was deeper, and where it was much easier to fish. In my swim, I tended to catch most of my fish from very close to the near margin, so I always pitched my bivvy right back at the edge of the forest, and kept very quiet so as not to disturb the fish which were often very close to me. For a lot of French anglers, fishing is a very social activity, involving many visits from friends, and stealth does not seem to be something that they use a lot, so they normally fish at range, which probably explains why they seldom fished in my swim. That`s not to say that I look down on the French fishermen, far from it, and I have met some fantastic French anglers, but they just seem to have a different mind-set to me. They are very friendly and love company, whereas I`m happiest when I`ve got the lake to myself.

It had been warm and sunny all morning, so I couldn`t believe it when during the short drive to Contre, it started to rain. I hoped that it was just a short shower so that I`d be able to set up in the dry, but unfortunately the rain became heavier, and it was to last for the rest of the day, and into the night. My friend Vincent, who owned the lake, had told me that I was the only person fishing there, for the first part of the week at least, so I was very surprised when I drove down the track, to see what looked like a car parked near to the far end of the Middle Lake, and when I arrived at the swim, I just couldn`t believe my eyes.

The forest was gone!

The trees had all been felled, and there were several men working there, sawing the trees into logs, and stacking the logs into piles. There was a track where I used to pitch my bivvy, and just a ten yard strip of grass next to the lake remained untouched. I was absolutely devastated because the swim that I loved had been totally destroyed. My first reaction was to turn around, and go to fish elsewhere, but in the end I decided to stay and see what happened. I had six days fishing in front of me so I could afford to try here for a couple of days, and then to move elsewhere if it didn`t work out. I would have to pitch my bivvy very close to the water's edge, because there was a track where I normally pitched it, which was obviously used a lot by vehicles to access the old forest area, as they worked on the wood. None of this was going to help me to catch fish from this swim, especially as I normally caught them from so close to the near margin. The lake had always been fairly difficult, as the stock of carp was very low, probably about thirty in fifteen to twenty acres, and there was a lot of natural food for the fish in the lake, but all this was going to make the fishing much harder than normal.

As I started to set up my bivvy, the elastic in the poles snapped in two places. It was an Aqua M3 Duo bivvy, and with the overwrap, I hadn`t had much change out of a thousand pounds, when I bought it less than a year before, so you can imagine my thoughts when that happened. As I tried to join the sections of the poles together, I was really struggling. I joined two sections together, but when I tried to join the next section, the first joint came apart. The rain was absolutely pouring down now and I was becoming more and more frustrated. It must have taken me at least an hour to finally get the bivvy erected, a process that used to take me about five minutes, and it was perhaps just as well that there weren't any representatives from Aqua about at the time, because they would probably have found themselves suspended from the nearest tree – by the neck.

Well maybe not, because the trees had all been cut down!

What a start to my session!

I had a quick lead around, and I discovered that there was far less weed present than normal, which meant that I'd be able to fish with slack lines. I think that the long winter and cold spring, that they'd suffered in this part of Picardie, had caused this lack of weed-growth in most of the lakes at the time, but I was in no doubt that as the warmer weather arrived, the situation would soon change. I found some nice areas to fish to, and soon had them baited, and the rods in position. I started with tigernuts on two rods and pop-up's on the other two, and I would then see how things panned out, before deciding how to approach it during the rest of my time here.

As I watched the water, I thought that I saw a couple of fish, but I couldn't be sure. With the wind and rain, it made fish-spotting very difficult, but it raised my spirits a little bit anyway.

Just after eight o'clock that evening I saw a rat swimming across the surface of the lake, towards the right of my swim, and as I watched, I saw it dive. A few seconds later I heard a series of bleeps from my right-hand delkim and the indicator rose to the rod butt.

Great!

Not!

I retrieved the rig, which was fortunately not attached to a rat, and re-casted. I had been using tigernuts on that rod, with a small funnel-web bag of chopped tigers, but the re-cast was without the pva bag this time.

It was dark at about half past nine, and I was soon tucked up inside my sleeping bag, where I stayed until I heard a series of bleeps from my remote, just before half past eleven. It was my third rod this time, on which I was using a pop-up on a hinged stiff rig, and when I reached the rod, the indicator was tight to the butt. I picked up the rod, but instead of being attached to a carp as I had expected, there was nothing there at all.

Another rat?

I re-casted the rod as best that I could, but it was very dark and I couldn`t see the small tree on the far bank that I had used as a marker to direct the cast, but fortunately it seemed to go back ok.

I woke at first light on Monday morning, to find that the rain had stopped and it looked like being quite a pleasant day, although it was still rather cold. I re-casted my third rod, the one that I had casted in the dark, but I left the other three in position. Then I got myself some breakfast, which went down well with my first cup of coffee of the day.

As I sat and watched the water for the next couple of hours, I saw no signs of any carp at all. The only good thing was that there was no-one working behind me, and I hoped that perhaps they only worked there during the week-ends, and that they`d leave me in peace today. Unfortunately that wasn`t the case, and at about half past eight that morning I saw a tractor driving along the track towards me. It stopped just twenty yards behind me, and the driver then started operating a contraption which was attached to the back of his tractor, which split the tree-trunks into smaller logs.

Bang, bang, bang, bang, bang!

What small chance that I`d had of catching a carp from this swim seemed to be disappearing fast. I should have moved, but for some reason I decided to stay where I was for at least one more day. I certainly wasn`t happy though. Normally I could have gone to one of the lakes at Loeuilly, but they had all been fished heavily during the Enduro, which had taken place there during the previous few days, so I doubted that they would fish well for some time. The lake at Albert could only be night-fished for three nights per week, which were Friday, Saturday and Sunday, so that was out of the question too. I could have moved to the opposite end of the lake, away from all of the disturbance, and that`s probably what I should have done, but that part of the lake is fished much more heavily by the local anglers, and I didn`t like it so much. My other option was to move to the First lake at Contre, but that wasn`t a lake that I enjoyed fishing very much, so I stayed put. The broken elastic in my bivvy poles meant that setting up the bivvy again would be a real chore, but I decided that if things hadn`t improved by the next morning, then I`d just have to bite the bullet, and move.

When I`d set up the previous afternoon, I`d baited the spots that I was going to fish very lightly, but I'd also baited an area about thirty yards along the south bank, with fifteen handfuls of peanuts and about forty boilies. I hadn`t fished that area at all overnight, but with all the disturbance behind me, I thought that now might be a good time to try it, so I positioned a pop-up just my side of the bait. I also re-positioned my third rod about ten yards further out, so I now had three out of my four rods fishing at thirty yards or more from the near margin and only one close to me. This was not the way that I`d previously been successful fishing this swim, but needs must, and I hoped that it might help.

59

I saw no signs of any carp and it was much colder than it had been over the previous few days, so it came as a big surprise to me when I heard my left-hand delkim go into melt-down, at about eleven o'clock that morning. It was the rod that I had re-positioned earlier, on the edge of the bed of bait near the south bank, and when I picked up the rod I found myself connected to a carp. It felt like a very good fish, and I was slowly easing it towards me, when the hook-hold failed, and it was gone. It was my first hook-pull of the year, so you can imagine how I felt.

I threw another six handfuls of peanuts and twenty-five boilies over the area, and then got the hook-bait back into position. I'd hooked a fish at last, but one on the bank would be nice.

There were now a van and a car parked behind me, in addition to the tractor, and five men were working. Two men were sawing and splitting the tree trunks into logs, while the others were stacking them, so I knew that I wasn't going to get any peace and quiet for some time.

It didn't warm up at all during the afternoon and I sat there wearing a fleece and a thick coat and hat. By four o'clock it was so cold that I decided to get into my sleeping bag to keep warm, and I must have dropped off to sleep, because the next thing that I knew it was a quarter past five, and I was woken by a screaming delkim. It was the second rod this time, on which I was using a tigernut snowman, just ten yards from the near margin. The fish put up a tremendous scrap, but I played it very carefully, because I didn't want a repeat of the hook-pull that I'd suffered that morning. The carp swam up and down the margin in front of me, but I wasn't able to bring it to the surface for more than twenty minutes. It then surfaced once, before powering away to my left again. It was a good mirror, and all the time I was praying that the hook would hold. Fortunately the pressure finally told, and I was able to slide it over the net cord. I fastened the net to the bank with a bank-stick, and then punched the air with delight.

At last I had a smile on my face!

I set up the camera and centred the picture on a bank-stick, which I`d placed just behind the mat. That seemed fine, but I took a couple of test shots just to make sure, with me kneeling behind the mat, with my arms outstretched, as if I was holding a fish. It always makes my friends laugh, when they look at the photos on my camera, and they see a picture of me holding fresh air. The test shots were perfect, so I picked up the sling, and walked towards the margin, to wet it and to zero the scales. As I did so, my foot caught in the camera lead, and pulled the camera and tripod over, onto the floor.

What a clumsy idiot I am!

Fortunately the camera was fine, but I had to go through the whole process of setting up the camera again.

The Mirror weighed 31 lbs.7 oz. and was a lovely fish. As I was taking the photos, two of the workers came to watch, and they said that the fish was 'énorme'.

I returned the fish to the lake, sorted everything out, and then I returned to my bivvy, but I wasn`t there long when I had another take, on my left-hand rod this time. There wasn`t any need for the camera however, because the culprit was a tench.

I re-casted the rods for the night at about half past seven, all with various pop-up`s, and then after having a quick bite to eat, I climbed back into my sleeping bag again, to keep warm.

I woke at six o`clock on Tuesday morning, just as it was getting light. The night had been very quiet, with not a bleep from the delkims. I had seen a couple of fish just before dusk, but they were some distance away in the middle of the lake, and I hadn`t seen anything since. I left the baits in position for another couple of hours, but without success, so I re-casted them all with different rigs and baits. I put tigernuts on two of the rods and pop-ups on the others, and then I baited lightly over each one. The wind was now blowing from a westerly direction, straight towards the bivvy, which normally would have been good, but it felt quite cold, so I wasn`t sure.

At eleven o`clock I had a take on my right-hand rod. It felt quite small and I thought that it was probably another tench at first, but when I got it closer to me it seemed to wake up, and I realised that it was definitely another carp. A short while later my second carp of the session was safely in the net. It was a nice little mirror of 12 lbs.8 oz. and I had just finished taking the photos and returned the fish, when it started to rain. It was only a short shower, but the rain was quite heavy, and I was forced to dive into the bivvy and zip down the door. If that shower had arrived just a few minutes earlier, I would have been soaked.

Perhaps my luck was changing.

Disappointingly, the afternoon produced no more fish to my rods, and I didn`t see any signs of carp at all. Then at about eight o`clock that evening, the wind dropped leaving the surface of the lake flat calm, and during the next hour or so I must have seen more than twenty carp. Of course some of these were probably the same fish that I had seen several times, but there were definitely a lot of carp in the area. The fish were head-and-shouldering, bubbling, and sometimes even jumping clear of the water. Most of this activity was at about fifty or sixty yards from me, which was probably about twenty yards from my nearest hook-bait, but an occasional fish showed a little closer. As I sat and watched, I was sure that something just had to happen, but an hour later I hadn't heard a single bleep from my delkims.

At one stage I even checked to see if the remote was switched on.

I could have re-casted one or more of my rods towards the main area of activity, but I thought that it would probably spook the fish, so I sat on my hands and waited.

At five past nine it happened.

There were no warning bleeps, just a one-toner, and my right-hand rod was away. It was a very powerful fish and I played it very carefully, but it was staying very close to the right-hand margin. In that corner of the lake there are a lot of bushes and snags, so I tried to slowly ease it to my left, away from trouble, but the more I tried, the more the carp kited towards that corner. When the fish was five yards from the snags I realised that desperate measures were called for, or else I was going to lose it, so I held on tight with the rod fully compressed, hoping that I could prevent it going any further right. All seemed to be going well and I had gained a couple of yards of line, when out came the hook. It was my second hook-pull of the year, and two in two days.

Gutted!

There wasn't much daylight left, so I walked the rod along the bank and put the line in the clip. I checked the hook, which didn't seem too bad, but I gave it a few touches with the sharpening stone just to make sure, and then I put it straight back out. I thought that I'd had my chance and blown it, but unbelievably, five minutes later the same rod was away again. As you can imagine I played this fish very

very carefully, but this time I had no problem at all in guiding the fish where I wanted it to go, almost like a dog on a lead.

'Why couldn't I have done the same to the last fish?' I thought to myself.

It took some time, but eventually I drew it over the net cord, and punched the air. That capture felt so good, after losing the last fish. It was a mirror of twenty-five pounds exactly, and although it wasn't as big as some of the other carp that I'd caught recently, it meant a lot to me.

It was dark by this time, so I put the carp in a sack, which I carefully placed in the deep margin, so that I could get some good photos in the morning. I re-casted the rod but I couldn't see the small tree that I used as a sight marker, because it was just too dark. I'd re-cast it again at first light to make sure that it was perfectly on the spot.

The next morning was totally uneventful and I saw no signs of any carp at all, totally different from the previous evening. I took the rods out at one o'clock that afternoon and drove to the supermarket in Conty for supplies. When I returned at two o'clock it was a lot warmer, but there was a moderate south-westerly wind which made it difficult for me to get the hook-baits back into position. Eventually I was happy with them, and I went back to my bivvy for some lunch – Fresh French bread with St. Agur cheese.

Delicious!

I intended to re-cast my rods at about half past seven that evening, but just before six o'clock I saw a lot of dark clouds on the horizon, so thinking that there was about to be a period of heavy rain, I decided to re-cast the rods straight away, before the rain started. The wind was still quite strong, and blowing from left to right, but I managed to position the hook-baits reasonably well, and then hurried back to my bivvy.

So far I had identified two definite feeding periods. The first was around eleven o`clock in the morning, and the second was between about eight o`clock in the evening and dusk. Unfortunately the heavy rain that I had expected arrived at about half past seven, and it just about put paid to the evening feeding period. It had been very quiet all day, and I hadn`t seen a single fish, so I was hoping for one that evening, but it seemed that it was not meant to be.

Perhaps in the morning.

There`s always hope.

Nothing happened overnight, and when I woke on Thursday morning it was cold and showery, which was not what I wanted. It was still only April, and some warm sunshine to raise the water temperature would have helped a lot, but there didn`t seem to be much chance of that happening. I re-casted the rods at about half past eight that morning, all with tigernut hook-baits. I had hooked five carp so far, and four of them had been on tigernuts, so it seemed like a sensible idea.

The workers were back behind me again that morning, sawing and splitting the wood, and generally making a lot of noise. After they hadn`t worked on Tuesday, I had hoped that they might leave me in peace, but they`d been back two days in a row now, so it looked like I`d just have to put up with it, but it certainly wasn`t helping matters.

Just before ten o`clock I saw several sets of bubbles between my third and fourth rod, and then I saw a big fish crash out about thirty yards past my right-hand rod. I had hooked two carp at about eleven o`clock over the last two days, so these sightings really encouraged me. Alexi came to see me at about half past ten, and we stood at the back of my swim watching the activity, We both thought that one of my rods would surely go, but eleven o`clock came and went without any further action. There were still the occasional few bubbles, but nowhere near as much activity as there had been, and I couldn`t help but think that my chance had gone. The workers had been exceptionally noisy during the last hour or so, and that had probably contributed to my lack of action. There wasn`t much that I could do about that however, other than to hope that they wouldn`t return the next day. There were now just two more days left of my session, and I hoped that I`d be able to add another carp or two to my tally.

I saw very little during the rest of the day and that evening I decided to re-position two of my rods at longer range. My third rod was cast to an area about fifty yards or so from me, in an area that I had seen fish earlier in the session, and my left-hand rod was casted about the same distance up south bank. Unfortunately I didn`t see any signs of carp at all that evening, despite having a very good view of the majority of the lake, and I went to sleep that night without much hope of any more carp, but at least I`d get a good night's sleep. I was right in that the night was very quiet, but I was unexpectedly woken at half past five the next morning by a screaming delkim. It was my third rod, which I had re-positioned the previous evening. I was fishing with the clutch on that reel set fairly tight, but despite that, when I reached the rod the line was out of the clip and the spool was turning, which left me in no doubt that a carp was responsible. When I picked up the rod I was immediately forced to back-wind as the fish took at least thirty yards of line, as it powered away from me. I then tried to ease it back towards me but it was having none of it, and it went on another long run to my left. I then started to slowly bring the fish back towards me. After about five minutes, I had managed to re-gain the line that the fish had taken, and I seemed to be gaining some sort of control, when the line went slack. I don`t know about you, but whenever I suffer a hook-pull I always reel in fast, hoping that the fish had just swum towards me. Normally that isn`t the case, and I just reel in a rig, with no carp. This time however, that is exactly what had happened, and after reeling in about ten yards of line, I came back into contact with the fish.

What a relief!

Strangely, after that I was able to bring the fish towards me quite easily, until it was about ten yards in front of me, and then it was a different matter altogether. The carp stayed deep and went on several runs, first to my left and then to my right. It must have been more than twenty minutes into the fight before I caught my first glimpse of the carp, as I saw it just under the surface. It looked like a good common, but it wasn`t beaten yet, and it went on another run out into the lake again, taking over twenty yards of line. I slowly eased it back towards me but it was at least another five minutes before I was able to bring it to the surface again. It looked beaten now, and I took a big step into the lake, to make netting the fish easier in the deeper water. I slid the carp along the surface towards the waiting net, and finally it was almost over the net cord. The fish didn`t seem to like the look of the net however, and with a kick of its tail, it turned and powered away from me again. Over five minutes later I was still trying to bring the carp back to the surface.

'That`s ridiculous' I thought, 'Five minutes ago it was beaten! It can`t fight much more surely!'

Finally I brought the fish to the surface once more, and this time as I slid it towards me, I was able to lift the net around it.

I was absolutely delighted, and after I had secured the net with a bank-stick, I raised both of my arms above my head in triumph. That looked to be a good fish, and a common too, which made it all the better. Nearly all of the carp that I had caught from this lake in the past had been mirrors, with just one common before this.

It was just getting light by this time, so I decided to sack the carp for a couple of hours, so that I could take some photos in decent light. I went to the car to get my mat, my sling and a sack, and then I set up my scales on my tripod, zeroed the sling, and put a bucket of water and my forceps next to the mat. I cut the line close to the rig, and then carried the fish to the mat in the net. When I opened the mesh to look at my prize, I was amazed to see that it wasn't a common at all, but a mirror. It was very light in colour and very long and thin, which is why I had mistaken it for a common, but what a lovely fish it was!

After un-hooking and weighing the carp, which was 26 lbs.7 oz, I put it into the sack and placed it in a deep part of the margin to my right. Then I made myself some breakfast and some coffee, and sat there watching the water totally content.

A couple of hours later, I was about to do the photos, when a couple of French anglers arrived, and they walked around the lake to see me. They couldn't speak a word of English, but my french is quite good, so we managed to understand one another reasonably well. One of them offered to take the photos of my fish for me, and although he obviously wasn't exactly an expert with the camera, he was able to get some good shots. I told him to take a lot of photos from different distances, and although some weren't very good, with the top of my head chopped off, or the tail of the fish not in the picture etc, there were some that were very good indeed, and some that I could improve on my computer when I got home.

I thanked them both for their help, and then we discussed the lakes. They had never fished here before, and they didn`t know which of the lakes to try. I told them that there were fish to a good size in both of the lakes, but that this one was the more difficult of the two and with a lower stock. I then suggested that as they were undecided which lake to fish, that they might consider doing what I had seen several other anglers do in the past. If they set up their bivvies about half-way along this lake, where the two lakes were only twenty yards apart, they would be able to cast two rods into this lake and two rods into the other, and fish them both. They liked that idea a lot, and after we had wished each other 'Bonne Pêche', they walked back to do just that.

The rest of the day was very uneventful, but that evening conditions seemed quite good, and I was expecting to see a few fish. Unfortunately I saw none at all and the lake seemed totally lifeless. During my last night on the lake I didn`t hear a single bleep from my delkims, and the next morning I started packing up feeling just a little disappointed with what I`d caught. Six carp hooked in six days is a fairly good result on this lake, which is far from easy, but those two hook-pulls made a big difference.

That would be my last proper fishing trip until the end of July, because I had planned to go on holiday with my wife. We were to go touring France with the caravan for two months, which we were both really looking forward to, but unfortunately it meant that I wouldn`t be able to fish from mid-May until Mid- July. When I say that I wouldn`t be able to fish during this time, that isn`t quite true. I would be taking a small telescopic rod and a few bits of tackle with me, so I`d probably be able to grab an odd few hours fishing from time to time, but that's about all. Any more than that and my wife wouldn't be happy. She allows me to fish almost as much as I like, most of the time, so I thought that it was only fair that these couple of months should be a proper holiday, rather than just a fishing trip.

I was determined however, to make up for it when we returned.

CHAPTER SEVEN – EN VACANCES

We travelled down to Kent on Wednesday 20th May and stopped at a site just ten minutes from the channel tunnel. We stayed there overnight, and early the next morning travelled through the tunnel, just before eight o`clock, and we were soon in France. It was quite a long way to Lez-Eaux, which was where we were to stay for the first five days of our holiday, but we took our time, stopping twice on the way, and we arrived at mid-afternoon, after a very pleasant and easy drive. In no time at all we had the caravan all set up, and dinner was on the table. The sun was shining out of a clear blue sky and it really was rather pleasant, which was certainly very different to the weather that we had suffered the previous day back in England. It had rained almost non-stop while we were in Kent, and I`d been wearing a fleece and turned up the heating in the caravan to keep warm. There was no need for a fleece here though, and certainly no need to turn on the heating either, in fact we had all the windows open to try to keep cool.

There is a small fishing pond at Lez-Eaux, which I had fished on my previous visits there, so after dinner I walked over to have a look – as you do. The pond contains quite a few common carp, which are quite long and thin in shape, and they remind me of the wild common carp that we used to catch in England many years ago. These carp are not enormous. They average about five or six pounds, with the biggest probably reaching just into double figures, but they are beautiful fish, and they put up a real scrap, especially on the light tackle that I would be using. Most of the pond is covered in lily pads, which makes it quite difficult to land the fish, and when they are hooked the carp tend to swim straight into the thickest pads that they can find.

When I arrived at the pond there were two people fishing. They were an Englishman and his wife and I asked them how it was going, but the answer that they gave me wasn't quite what I wanted to hear. They said that the fishing was very slow and that they had only caught one carp all week, despite fishing almost every day. They were using floating crust and they said that they normally caught quite a few fish with this method, but the fishing was not as good as usual, probably because it had been so cold recently. France had suffered a cold start to the year, just as England had. It was quite warm now though, and the forecast was for more warm dry weather to come, so hopefully things would soon improve. We talked for ten minutes or so, and then I wished them luck and went back to join Anita and open the first bottle of wine of the holiday.

The next day we went to the coast, which wasn't far away and our dog Stan went swimming in the sea for the first time. We weren't sure if he'd like the salt water, but he loved every minute of it. We then went to a local restaurant and I had 'moules frites' – mussels and chips, which was delicious, especially washed down with some ice cold beer.

That evening I decided to fish the carp pond for the first time this trip, just for a couple of hours or so, just before dark. I set up the little telescopic rod that I'd brought with me and attached a light pole float and a small hook. The pole float was far from ideal, because they are not designed to be casted with a rod and line, and they are normally just lowered into the water from the end of a pole. When used on a rod and line they are very prone to tangling, but it was all that I had with me, so it would have to do. I used sweetcorn as bait and fed little and often. In the past when I have fished here before and fed sweetcorn in this way, the swim soon resembled a jacuzzi with bubbles everywhere, but this time there were very few bubbles at all. After about an hour and a half I hadn't had a single bite and I needed to go to the loo, which was about seventy or eighty yards away. I know that I shouldn't have done it, but I left the float in the water while I went. I was only away for about a minute, but when I got back there was no sign of my float and my line was far to the left of my swim. I retrieved my float but the line had broken at the hook-link. Leaving my tackle in the water while I was away was a very stupid and irresponsible thing to do, but to receive my only bite so far in the one minute that I was away from my rod was also rather unlucky.

I tied on a new hook-link and tested the float for depth. I wanted to set it about an inch or so over-depth so that my hook-bait would just rest on the lake-bed. To do this I put a large split-shot just above the hook. This shot was heavy enough to sink the float unless it was resting on the lake-bed. I then set the float at too shallow a depth so that the float sank, and then I increased the distance of the float from the hook, until the float no-longer sank. Unbelievably, on my second trial cast, a carp took the shot that I had placed just above the hook, but as it swam away from me the hook pulled.

That was now two carp that I'd hooked, and I'd lost them both!

Not a good start.

About an hour later my float slid away and I hooked another. I applied strong pressure to try to stop the carp from going too deep into the pads, but the hook-link snapped.

Three hooked, and three lost.

This was just getting worse.

That was my last action of the day and I packed feeling rather dispirited.

The next afternoon I started fishing just after three o'clock in the same swim. Very little happened at first, but at about half past four I saw lots of bubbles all around my float, and I just knew that I was going to get a take. About five minutes later, away went the float and I hooked a carp which swam powerfully deep into the lilies and the line snapped like cotton. My main-line was 5 lbs. breaking-strain maxima, but the four feet of line below this was only 2 lbs. breaking-strain, and that was clearly not strong enough.

I set up again, but this time I used stronger tackle. I used the 5 lbs. mainline straight through to a 4 lbs. hook-link, and hoped that this would hold firm against the lilies. Not surprisingly, the loss of that fish had scared the others, and nothing much happened for quite some time. Gradually though, I began to see more and more bubbling, and by seven o'clock that night there were bubbles everywhere. Just before half past seven my float slid away, and I hooked my second carp of the day. Once again I wasn't able to stop it reaching the lilies, although so far the line hadn't snapped, so I still had a chance. The carp must have been at least ten feet into the pads on my left and was still pulling hard, but gradually I managed to ease it out, and into open water. That didn't last long however, and the carp then dived into the pads on my right. I tried to stop it but there was no chance, and it kept going deeper and deeper into the pads. Despite this, I was still in contact with the fish, and inch by inch I worked it back towards me. It took some time, but about five minutes later I was finally able to draw it over the net cord. I left the fish in the net and quickly ran the 200 yards to the caravan to get Anita, who followed me back to the lake with the camera, where she took several photos of me with the carp. It was a beautiful common of about eight or nine pounds, and had given me an incredible scrap.

Fantastic!

On my last day at Lez-Eaux I went for just an hour or so in the evening, arriving at about half past seven. I had bought a few hooks to nylon from the local supermarket, which were made with 5 lbs mono, and I hoped that this stronger hook-link would help to combat the pads. I baited little and often with sweetcorn and bubbles soon started to appear. After half an hour or so I hooked a carp which soon sought the sanctuary of the pads. My stronger tackle served me well however, and I was able to bring the carp out of the pads into open water.

'That's the hard part done' I thought, but I was wrong, and as I guided the carp towards the waiting net, the hook pulled.

Not to be deterred, I threw a few more grains of sweetcorn into the swim and followed them with my float and baited hook. Despite losing a fish just a short time before, there were still fish feeding in the swim, and about twenty minutes later I hooked another. Once again the carp dived deep into the pads, but I was able to extract it without too much trouble and a minute or so later I had a lovely little common of about six pounds in the net.

That was enough for me. I had achieved what I had set out to do, so I packed up and walked back to the caravan to tell Anita about my success. We were moving to another site the next morning which was just over one hundred miles further south. Apparently there was a lake at that site too, so I would see how I fared there.

We arrived at Chateau du Deffay on Tuesday afternoon, and the site was idealic. There was a beautiful lake of about 15 acres surrounded by a forested area, and there were flowers and wildlife everywhere. Dominic, the owner, told me that the lake didn't contain any carp, but that there were plenty of tench, bream and various other small fish.

Despite the lack of carp, the lake looked so appealing that I decided to give it a try, and I fished for a couple of hours on the second evening. After an hour or so I had caught three or four roach, when a man came and stood next to me, watching me fish. We talked for a while and he told me that he was Romanian. He was working in France at the time and staying in one of the chalets on the site. He said that he would bring me luck and that I would soon catch a big fish. The words had hardly left his mouth when my float slid under and I hooked something much larger than the roach that I'd caught before. My Romanian friend thought that the fish was enormous, and he tried to tell me how to play it.

'Take your time because it is a very big fish' he said. 'Don't pull too hard or you will lose it'.

It was a bream of about a pound and a half, and he was delighted with it. I didn't have the heart to tell him that I had caught carp to almost fifty pounds only a couple of months before, so I wasn't quite so impressed with this bream as he was. He was even more surprised when I returned the fish to the lake.

'Don't you eat them?' he said.

I must admit that just the thought of eating a slimy bream almost turned my stomach.

The next evening I went back to try again, for a couple of hours just before dark, and I had caught a few roach and rudd when my Romanian friend joined me once again.

'I have come to bring you luck again' he said. 'I think that you will catch another big fish'.

As we watched, my float slid under, and I soon landed another bream of about the same size as the one that I'd caught the previous day.

'Please don`t put it back' my friend said. 'I would love to have a fish like that.'

'Do you really eat bream?' I asked in astonishment.

'Oh yes, they are very nice' he replied. 'Very sweet.'

So I gave him the bream and he was so pleased that you would have thought that I`d given him the world. He took it back to his chalet, and told me that he would eat it for his supper the next day. A short time afterwards I caught another bream, but this one was even bigger at about 2½ - 3 lbs. That was enough for me and I packed up and went back to the caravan.

I didn`t fish the next evening, and the following day we moved to another site further south near to Chatellerault. There was no lake on this site, but it was beautiful there and we spent four days just relaxing and swimming in the swimming pool. With the occasional glass of wine too, of course.

Our next stop was further south again, not far from Bordeaux at St. Emillion. It was another lovely site, amongst the vineyards of one of the most famous wine-growing areas of France, and while we were there we sampled some of the St. Emillion Grand Cru wine, which was delicious.

There was a lake of about 25 acres on the site which was reputed to hold carp to a good size, so it wasn`t long before I had a walk round to investigate. It was well over 30 degrees at the time and the sun was blazing down out of a clear blue sky, so I didn`t expect to see much, but I did find an area that I fancied fishing later that evening.

I arrived at my chosen swim at about eight o`clock that evening, and after plumbing for depth I started to introduce some feed. First I soaked some bead which I then mashed up with my hands and threw into the swim. I hoped that this would leave an attractive carpet of breadcrumbs on the lake-bed, and I then fed sweetcorn, little and often, over the top.

After a while I saw three or four carp crash out, near to the right-hand tree-line, and then I saw several large patches of bubbles, which I hoped were caused by feeding carp. These bubbles appeared in several different places while I was there, but they were never quite close enough to me, and were always just a few yards further out than I could cast with my light tackle. I just couldn't quite reach them and I packed up after a frustrating couple of hours, having just caught two small roach.

The next day was incredibly hot, with temperatures reaching 36 degrees, but even so, eight o'clock saw me back in the same swim to try again. Initially I baited heavily with bread and then little and often with sweetcorn as before. Once again I saw three carp crash out and I also saw several large patches of bubbles. This time however, some of the bubbles were near where I'd thrown the bread, and were within casting range.

After about half an hour my float slid away and I struck firmly, expecting to feel the resistance of a sizable carp on the end of the line, but unfortunately the culprit was only a roach of about half a pound. A few casts later my float disappeared again, but this time I was left in no doubt that I was attached to a carp at last, as the fish exited the swim with the clutch on my reel screaming in protest. The carp swam straight towards the margin on my right, which was about 50 yards away. When I had walked around the lake the previous day, I had noticed that there were a lot of roots and branches in the margins, and it was obviously these snags that the carp was heading for. I slowly increased the pressure on the fish, but it wasn't slowing it down much at all, and when it was about 5 yards short of the margin I realised that desperate measures were called for, so I clamped down hard, not giving any more line at all, and prayed that my light tackle would hold. To my surprise the fish turned and I was able to draw it out into open water again.

'Now I've got a chance' I thought.

I slowly brought the fish towards me, but as I did so, it started to kite into the near margin to my right. From my position, I wasn't able to do anything to stop this, so I started to move to my right. This wasn't easy because there were three large trees in my way and I had to pass the rod around each of them. Every time I did this the line went slack for a short time, which enabled the fish to get nearer to the margin. Eventually I reached a position level with the fish, but unfortunately it seemed to be snagged in some roots. I feared the worst at this point, but I applied some pressure and slowly but surely the fish started to move towards me. I could feel the line grating on the roots and was amazed that my light line had managed to withstand this treatment. I was just starting to think that I might win this battle after all, when the hook pulled and the carp was gone.

Surprisingly, I didn't feel too bad about the loss of that carp. It was obviously a sizeable fish, and with my light tackle the odds were stacked well in favour of the carp. At least I'd managed to hook a carp, and hopefully I'd land the next one.

After losing that fish the swim went quiet for a while, but about half an hour later I started to see bubbles appear on the surface again, near to my float. More and more bubbles appeared and then my float slid away again. It wasn't a carp this time though, and shortly afterwards I landed a bream of about two pounds. I un-hooked it in the water to save getting my net covered in bream slime, and then I re-casted and threw some more bread into the swim. I was sure that it was the bread that was attracting the fish, so a little more couldn't hurt.

About half an hour before dark I hooked another carp. The fish swam towards the right-hand margin, just like the last one, and once again I had great difficulty stopping it. I finally managed to turn it just short of the bank, and then it started to swim out towards the middle of the lake.

'That's a bit of luck' I thought. 'I don't mind it going out there, well away from all of the snags.'

But it wasn't all good news, because the carp just kept going further and further away from me, until when it was about 100 yards away, the hook came out. I don't think that I was applying too much pressure at the time; I was just letting it run in open water, so the hook-pull was a real disappointment.

As it was now approaching dusk, I packed up and made my way back to the caravan to tell Anita all about it. I was very hopeful however, that I'd be able to make up for my misfortune the following night.

Wednesday was scorching hot once again with temperatures reaching 35 degrees, but in the evening a moderate wind sprung up. This wind was blowing straight towards the swim that I had been fishing, and normally I would have thought that the wind in my face was a good thing in these hot conditions, but not with the tackle that I was using. I was fishing with a light pole float on my telescopic rod, because that was all that I had with me, and I couldn't cast it far with the wind in my face. I tried again and again, but I just couldn't reach the distance that I wanted to fish. Pole floats aren't meant to be fished on a rod and line, so they don't cast well at the best of times, but trying to cast it into the wind was a nightmare, and every other cast produced a tangle. I could have fished in a different part of the lake of course, where the wind was behind me. This would have helped my casting, but this was where the fish were and I had baited this swim for the previous two days, so I stayed where I was. I hoped that the wind would drop and give me a chance, but by half past nine the wind was even stronger if anything, so I packed up and returned to the caravan to drown my sorrows with a couple of glasses of wine.

The carp had definitely got the better of me at this lake, but I was sure that if I'd had any sort of decent carp tackle with me; it would have been a different story.

The next day we moved further south and I didn't get the chance to fish again for the rest of the holiday. We had a fantastic time though. The weather was fantastic, with temperatures of over thirty degrees almost every day and they even reached the low forties at one point. We visited some beautiful places, and enjoyed plenty of good food and wine, so it couldn't have been much better really. Our dog Stan went swimming every day, so he was happy too, despite the hot temperatures. Whenever he seemed to be a little too warm we either took him swimming or poured some water over him, and he was fine.

Just before we travelled back to England, we stopped at Amiens, and Corentin, Sophie and Benoit came to see us. Clément and Camille wanted to come too, but unfortunately when we were in Amiens, they were in the south of France on holiday, so they couldn't join us, but we raised a glass of wine to them in their absence.

Benoit told me about a lake he had heard about which was only about five or six miles from Amiens, so the next day we drove out to have a look. When we arrived, we discovered that there wasn't just one lake, there were five. There were several anglers pole-fishing on the first lake, which didn't seem a good sign to me, but further along the bank one angler was carp-fishing, so we stopped for a chat. What he told us seemed unbelievable. He said that there were mainly small carp in this lake, which is what I had first thought when I saw the other anglers fishing with a pole, but when we asked about the second lake he said that it contained some big carp. Now what some people think are big carp may not necessarily be the same as what we think are are big carp, so we asked him how big they were, and the answer left us stunned. He said that the largest was 30 kilos. Now 30 kilos is about 66 lbs. and I`d never caught a fish anywhere near to that weight. If this was true then we may just have stumbled onto something quite special. We asked if night fishing was allowed and he said that it was, so it really was looking good. We thanked him for his help and started to walk around the second lake. As we walked I told Benoit that it sounded tremendous, but I wasn`t sure if it was true. If there were carp of almost seventy pounds in that lake, then I would have expected it to be crowded with carp anglers, and it wasn`t.

As we walked we came across another couple of anglers, so we stopped and asked them about the lake, and these anglers told us a completely different story. They said that the carp were mainly low doubles and that the largest they had ever seen caught from there was about eighteen pounds. They also said that night fishing wasn`t allowed. Now that seemed more believable to me, but just to be sure we talked to another half a dozen anglers further round the lake and they all told the same story. The carp were mostly doubles and night fishing wasn`t allowed. We asked about the third lake, which looked very nice indeed. It was partly covered with lily pads and did look very carpy. Unfortunately we were told that there was no night fishing on that lake, so that was no good for us either.

We almost gave up and went back to Amiens at this point, but we decided that we might as well take a look at the last two lakes while we were there. These two lakes were a few hundred yards away from the other three, and were also quite a bit larger. The first lake looked quite good, but there were a lot of sailing boats moored there. In my experience, sailors and fishermen rarely get on well, when they`re on the same lake, so that put me off a bit. There was also no-one there to ask, so we walked on to have a look at the last lake.

When we arrived, we saw a man just leaving, so we asked him if he knew anything about the lake. He said that he didn`t know much, but that there was an angler fishing just along the bank that was a member and that he would help us. We walked along to talk to him and he couldn`t be more helpful. He said that the lake contained carp to just over 20 kilos (44 lbs.) as well as a few catfish, bream, tench roach and perch. Night fishing was allowed, but there was a three day rule. After fishing for three days you had to leave the lake and not return for at least a further three days. Now that rule wouldn`t be a problem because I could fish three days here and four days at Loeuilly or Contre, and that would make a good weeks fishing. He showed us his licence and told us all the rules, which seemed very sensible. He said that the lake was very rarely busy, especially mid-week. The lake was fishable on all banks, but a car could only be driven to the near bank on which we were standing. The other swims could be fished but we would need a barrow to get our tackle to the swims. This news made me take a greater interest in the swims on the far side of the lake. French fishermen tend to take a lot of tackle with them so would normally fish close to their cars, so that they didn`t have to carry it too far. I was sure that this meant that the far bank swims weren`t fished very often. Apparently the cost of a permit was 89 euros for the year which seemed very reasonable, so I made my mind up to get a permit and give this lake a try. The man told Benoit where the shop was in Amiens that we could buy a permit, and Benoit promised to take me there the next time that I came fishing to France.

We then had a walk around to the far bank and some of the swims that we found there looked very good indeed. As we walked back to the car I was very excited. It seemed as though we had found a lake that I would enjoy fishing, but it wouldn`t be until August at the earliest. I had already made plans to fish at Contre and Loeuilly on my next trip towards the end of July, but the following month I could hopefully fish here for three days.

After over two months without any serious fishing, I was gagging to get the carp rods out again.

CHAPTER EIGHT – JULY AT CONTRE

I arrived at Contre just after seven o`clock in the morning on Thursday 23$^{rd}$ July, and I was pleased to see that there wasn`t anybody fishing on either lake. I decided to fish on the middle lake, and chose the east bank swim, where I had fished earlier in the year. There were quite a lot of bubbles within ten yards of the bank where several carp were obviously feeding, which certainly raised my hopes, but I knew that it was probably quite weedy, so I was going to have to lead around quite a bit to find some suitable spots to place my hook-baits. I used a very light lead to do this, and I tried to cause as little disturbance as possible, but I knew that I`d probably scare those fish away. It took quite some time because there was even more weed than I had expected, but it had to be done. There was just no point in casting blind, and ending up with the hook-baits buried in weed. All the rods were clipped-up, and the spots were baited lightly with hemp, chopped tigers and a few chopped boilies, so I flicked the hook-baits into position, and I was fishing at last. As expected, the fish that had been feeding close to me had moved away a little, but hopefully they would return. It was a very hot day and as I sat there in the warm sunshine, I thought how good it was to be back.

Vincent came to see me just after midday and we talked for a while. He told me that the lakes at Tilloy were going to allow night-fishing next year, which was good news. I liked the look of those lakes and had wanted to fish there for some time, but the no night-fishing rule had made them a non-starter for me in the past. Vincent told me that just 50 season tickets were going to be issued, and only for locals, so it wasn`t likely that I`d be able to get a ticket myself, but both Vincent and Alexi would be members, so I might be able to fish there as their guest.

Vincent left at about one o`clock to go back to work, so I had something to eat and then sat to read for a while. I didn`t read for long though, because I started to feel very tired, I`d missed a night's sleep because I`d travelled overnight, so I thought I`d just lie down for half an hour, and close my eyes. A power nap I think they call it, but I slept for a lot longer than half an hour, and the next thing that I knew, it was six o`clock.

I reeled in the rods to re-cast, and I got quite a surprise. The tigernut hook-baits were fine, but the two pop-up`s certainly were not.

More than half of each pop-up had been eaten away by crayfish.

I had a cure for that problem however, and I spent the next few minutes encasing some pop-up`s with boilie mesh.

'Let`s see if the crayfish can deal with that' I said to myself.

I soon had all the hook-baits in position. I was using tigernuts on two rods and white pop-up`s on the other two. Both of those baits had been successful here for me in the past, so I hoped that they might work for me again.

At about nine o`clock the wind dropped and I started to see signs of carp. Not a lot. Just a few bubbles, and I saw one fish just break the surface, but it was very encouraging.

The night was very frustrating. I heard a few bleeps from my delkims, but nothing that I could definitely say was due to carp. I was in and out of my bivvy all night, every time that one of my delkims sounded, and I got very little sleep. In the morning I reeled in my left-hand rod, only to discover that the pop-up had been eaten away by crayfish, despite it having been covered in mesh. When I reeled in my right-hand rod I discovered that there was no bait at all, and that the hair had been bitten through. The pop-up on my third rod had been eaten away too, despite the mesh, and I wasn't sure what to do to solve this problem.

The only hook-bait that remained intact was the tigernut snowman on my second rod, so I thought that perhaps I should use tigernuts on all four rods for the next night. I did have some plastic boilies, which would have been perfect for this situation, but unfortunately I'd left them at home, because I didn't think that I'd need them here.

When the wind picked up at about mid-morning, it was from an easterly direction, so it was blowing away from me, and probably taking any carp in the area with it. Things certainly weren't looking good. I had always caught fairly consistently on this lake in the past, but I was now afraid that I was heading for a big fat blank.

It was very hot indeed in the afternoon, and now that all of the trees had been cut down at the back of the swim, there was nothing to offer any shade, so I just sat there and roasted. There were no signs at all of any carp, and my earlier fears that the fish would follow the new wind, and head to the opposite end of the lake, seemed to have come to fruition, but I'd find out for sure in the couple of hours before nightfall. If there were still any carp present, then they'd probably show themselves then.

Vincent stopped by on his way home from work, and I explained the problems that I'd had with the crayfish. He suggested a swim at the opposite end of the lake, and told me about some of the spots where I should place my hook-baits. It did sound good, but it was too late to move that evening, unless I wanted to set up in the dark, so I decided to stay where I was for the night. If tonight proved to be as bad as the previous one, then I'd move in the morning.

I re-casted the rods, all with tigernuts to try to avoid the crayfish, and then I watched the water until dark. I saw nothing, although there was a little bit of excitement at about half past nine, when I had a 'take' on my right-hand rod. There was nothing there when I picked up the rod, so I assumed that it wasn`t a carp that was responsible.

I didn`t introduce any more free bait, because I didn`t want to encourage any more crayfish into the area. There were enough of them out there already.

The night was very quiet and when I woke at seven o`clock the next morning, it was pouring with rain and a strong westerly wind was blowing it straight into my bivvy. I wouldn`t be moving in those conditions, so I zipped shut the bivvy door, and went back to sleep. When I woke again a couple of hours later, the strong westerly wind was still howling down the lake, but at least it had stopped raining, so I grabbed a quick bite to eat, and then started packing everything into the car.

By half past eleven my bivvy was up in my new swim on the peninsular at the western end of the lake. As I looked down the lake I had grave doubts that moving had been a good idea. Surely the carp would follow that strong wind, and if they did, they`d end up in the swim that I`d just moved from. It was too late to change my mind now however, so I`d just have to wait and see what happened.

I made a few casts with a light lead to the left of my swim, and I soon realised that there was a lot less weed here than in the east bank swim that I`d fished for the previous two days. I soon found a couple of decent spots, one just short of the willow and the other just short of a large far-bank bush. I baited these lightly with a dozen tigers and half a dozen boilies, and then I went to have a lead around at the front of the peninsular. Vincent had told me that he had caught several fish very close to the near bank at the front of the swim, and I soon found two spots that felt very good at about five yards range. I baited these two close spots with hemp, chopped tigers, and just a few chopped boilies. Once again there was very little weed here, which was a worry. Would carp really stay here, with very little weed, and with the wind blowing strongly towards the opposite end of the lake?

It seemed unlikely.

I didn't cast in straight away, deciding to wait to allow the swim to settle after the disturbance that I had caused. Instead I made myself something to eat. I hadn't realised how hungry I was until I started eating, but I soon felt much better. I finally positioned my hook-baits just after three o'clock in the afternoon. I used orange pop-ups on the two left-hand rods, one with a 360 rig and the other with a hinged stiff rig, both fished tight and using lead-clips and flying back-leads.

I used a different approach with the two rods at the front of the swim, where I fished with tigernuts on both rods and used light running leads on slack lines. Although it was still windy, at least the sun had come out and it was pleasantly warm.

Just before five o'clock I heard a series of bleeps from one of my delkims at the front of the swim, and when I reached the rod the hanger was tight to the butt.

'That didn't take long' I said to myself, but my jubilation didn't last long when I saw a sturgeon leap clear of the water on the end of my line. For a small fish it put up a decent scrap, and it was fully five minutes later before I was able to lift the net around it. I weighed the fish and the scales recorded a weight of 7 lbs.13 oz.

'At least I've caught a fish' I said to myself, but a sturgeon wasn't really what I wanted.

I re-casted the successful rod and sprinkled a little more hemp and chopped tigers around the hook-bait, before sitting back down to watch the water. Unfortunately I didn't see any signs of carp so I still wasn't sure about the swim. I re-casted the two rods to my left at about seven o'clock that night, one with a white pop-up, and the other with tigernuts, then I put a little more bait around each one. Not a lot, just a dozen boilies around the pop-up and a dozen tigernuts around the other hook-bait. I decided to leave the other two rods as they were for the night, and see what happened. I didn't want to make the mistake of putting too much bait in, but if I didn't catch anything during the night, I might add a little more bait the next day.

Overnight I heard three fish crash out, and although I couldn't tell if they were carp or sturgeon, I suspected that they were the latter. I heard the occasional single bleep from my delkims, probably caused by crayfish, but apart from that it was very quiet, so at least I was able to get a good night's sleep.

When I woke the next morning I was surprised to see an easterly wind blowing, completely the opposite direction to the previous day. This wind was blowing straight towards my swim, so I hoped that it would bring a carp or two with it.

Time would tell.

I reeled in my first rod to re-bait and re-cast, and I was disappointed to see that the 16 mm. white pop-up that I'd tied on the previous night, had been whittled away to less than a quarter of its original size. There were obviously a lot of crayfish here too, and that explained the single bleeps that I'd heard during the night.

For a change I tied on a cork-dust pop-up that matched my free-baits, and that had been soaked in bait dip for some time. I realised that this highly-flavoured bait may well attract the crayfish, but I hoped that they wouldn`t be quite so active during daylight hours, so I should get away with it. I thought that it should be very attractive to the carp, and would look more natural than the brightly coloured pop-up`s that I had used the previous day. I also attached a two-bait stringer and then catapulted eight more boilies around the hook-bait for good measure. I used an orange pop-up on a hinged stiff rig on the spot by the willow, and catapulted just eight boilies around it.

On the two close rods at the front of the swim I used little ten mm. pop-ups – one yellow and one washed-out pink. The pink one was a little too buoyant so I cut it in half, and that half-bait seemed to sit nicely just off the bottom, when I tested it. I then put some hemp, chopped tigers and chopped boilies around these hook-baits and sat back to see what happened.

Well what happened was absolutely nothing – not a single bleep from my delkims, so I decided that I had to do something. Out came the catapult and I put out fifty boilies and fifty tigernuts around both of my left-hand spots, and also a few more in a line between the two. Now you may think that that isn`t a lot of bait, and normally I would agree, but given the amount of crayfish in this lake, introducing that amount of bait could have been catastrophic. I knew that I may well regret doing it when night-time arrived and the crayfish came out to play, but I had to do something, because the way that I`d been fishing just hadn`t been working.

The wind dropped in the afternoon and it started to rain, so I was bivvy-bound for a while, which didn`t do much to raise my spirits, and I sat there wondering what else I could do. I'd now fished for three days on this lake in two different swims, and I didn't think that I'd even come close to catching a carp. In the past I'd always averaged about one carp per day here and I had never blanked, but it looked as though I might be leaving tomorrow with my tail firmly between my legs.

As the day went on, the temperature dropped and the rain got heavier. I was sitting in my bivvy wearing my full rain-gear with a woolly hat, and it was hard to believe that just a couple of days before it had been swelteringly hot, so hot in fact that I had to lie on top of my sleeping bag during the night to try to stay cool.

I re-casted my left-hand rod at five o'clock that evening. I used tigernuts on this rod and positioned them a lot closer to the bush than I had done previously, and I catapulted about twenty tigernuts around it.

Just after I had done this, the wind became much stronger. It was absolutely howling down the lake to such an extent that accurate casting was impossible, so I waited for the wind to drop before attempting to re-cast my other left-hand rod towards the willow. Several times during the next couple of hours or so, there was a slight lull in the wind, but each time, before I was able to cast, the wind started to blow just as hard again, and I had to wait. I finally managed to cast my second rod just after half past seven, more than two and a half hours after I had casted my first rod. I positioned the hook-bait, which was a white pop-up wrapped in boilie mesh, just 12 inches from the trailing branches of the willow, and I was very happy with the cast. I catapulted eight boilies around the hook-bait, and then went to re-cast the two rods at the front of the swim. These just required a little underarm flick, so I soon had them in position, one with tigernuts and the other with a critically-balanced bait. I sprinkled some hemp over both, and then returned to my bivvy, happy in the knowledge that all the hook-baits were positioned exactly as I wanted, and it was now up to the carp.

Well the carp decided not to play.

My last night at Contre was the quietest yet and I heard just two single bleeps all night, so I ended my session on the middle lake without hooking a single carp. That had never happened to me there before, and I just hoped that the main lake at Loeuilly would be better. I packed up the next morning, dodging the showers, and headed for the supermarket at Conty for supplies, before driving the short distance to Loeuilly.

CHAPTER NINE - BACK TO LOEUILLY

I arrived at Loeuilly just before midday, and as I drove down the track I could see that there was just one other angler on the lake. He was just setting-up on the point, so I chose a swim about 100 yards up the west bank, that I had last fished in April when I caught a 49 lbs.14 oz. mirror.

I set up the bivvy and then I put some boilies in a bucket of lake-water to soak for a couple of hours. As I was doing this, the other angler walked along the bank to talk to me. He couldn`t speak any English at all so we had to converse in French, and he told me that his brother would be arriving soon, and that he would want to cast his rods towards the far bank, in front of where I had pitched my bivvy. As you can imagine, I wasn`t happy about that at all, and I explained that I would be casting my rods there, and his brother would have to cast elsewhere.

With all of the lake to choose from, why did he want to cast in front of me?

How much of this got lost in translation, I`m not sure, but fortunately my friend Patrice arrived and when I explained the problem, he said that he`d have a word with the other angler. Patrice is six feet four inches tall so not many people argue with him, and sure enough, about ten minutes later he returned to my swim and told me that everything was ok. The other anglers had agreed that they would not cast past the large bush on the far bank, which left plenty of room for everyone. To be fair, the other anglers were very friendly after that, and we had no problems at all.

I made a few casts with a two ounce lead, and I soon found the spots that I wanted to fish to. There was a little more weed on them than before, but nothing that would cause me too many problems. There was quite a lot of weed however, closer to me, especially on the left-hand and middle positions, but I soon managed to clear the worst of it, so that I`d be able to bring a fish through the weed, should I manage to hook one.

You are allowed to use four rods here at Loeuilly, but I decided to use just three rods this time. There are some big fish in this lake, and using less rods meant that I could spread them apart slightly, which hopefully would reduce the chance of a hooked fish going over one of my other lines.

Once I was happy with the spots, I baited them all very heavily with boilies of two different sizes, which had been soaking in a bucket of lake water. The reason that I did this was because all of my spots were on quite soft silt, and I didn`t want the boilies to take on the smell of the silt. By soaking them, the boilies would take in some water, and I hoped that this would stop them from sucking in the smell of the silt quite so much. It`s something that I often do when I fish over silt. I can`t prove whether it helps or not, but I`ve been quite successful when I`ve done this, so it gives me confidence, which can`t be a bad thing.

After I`d sticked out the boilies, I sat down and had something to eat. It was now four o`clock in the afternoon, and I was starving. The food made me feel a lot better, and I started to prepare the rigs and hook-baits that I`d be using. I didn`t just tie three rigs however, instead I made quite a few, so that if I caught some carp during the night I'd have a new rig ready to cast. If nothing happened during the night, I`d have some rigs ready for the morning, so they wouldn`t be wasted.

I decided to use orange pop-ups on 360 rigs on two of my rods, and a snowman rig on the other, but I also tied up a rig with some tigernuts. There are quite a few grass carp in this

95

lake and tigernuts have accounted for several of them for me, so I'd probably try them in the morning.

There was a moderate to strong southerly wind blowing, which was right to left as I stood facing the lake, and some of the gusts were very strong indeed, so it made accurate casting very difficult, but fortunately all three hook-baits went in fine.

I'd just casted the last rod, when one of the other anglers walked down the bank to tell me that he'd caught two carp. They weren't very big, but he was very pleased with them. He told me that they were both mirror carp and they weighed 8 kilos and 15 kilos, which is about 17 lbs. and 33 lbs. He asked me if I'd caught anything, but I explained that I'd just casted in. To be honest, I didn't really expect much to happen until the next day at least, because I'd baited very heavily. I had four days fishing in front of me, so I could afford to wait. I have often found that when I have baited heavily, like I had here, that the session normally starts very slowly, but then it gets better as time goes by, with each day being better than the last, as the fish get on the bait.

At about eight o'clock that evening four anglers arrived, and they parked their cars a few yards up the bank from me. They asked me where I had casted my rods, because they wanted to fish to my right.

'Oh no, not again' I thought.

I told them where I was fishing, and explained where they could cast their rods, but said that they wouldn't have much room, especially because there were four of them. I then told them that there was no-one fishing in the top half of the lake, so they would have much more room if they fished there. They liked that idea, thanked me and wished me 'Bonne Peche', before driving to the top part of the lake, while I breathed a big sigh of relief.

Nothing much happened during the night, although I did hear several single bleeps from my delkims, which I put down to fish moving through the weed on my side of the hook-baits. These fish were not necessarily carp, and could just as easily have been bream.

I reeled in all the rods to re-cast at seven o`clock in the morning, and I was very pleased to see that all the hook-baits were in perfect condition, with not a mark on them from the attentions of crayfish, which made a pleasant change after my experiences at Contre.

I decided to re-cast each rod with a different hook-bait – one with tigernuts, one with a pop-up and the last rod with a snowman rig. All three of these presentations had worked well for me here in the past, so giving the carp several different options seemed like a good idea. After re-casting the rods, I retreated to the bivvy for some breakfast.

During the morning I heard my delkims bleep on two occasions. First the hanger on my left-hand rod lifted a couple of inches. I was unsure whether I should hit it or not, but because I had no further indication at all, I just slackened off the line a little, so that the hanger fell back to its original position, and I left it. I decided that if it happened again on that rod however, then I wouldn`t leave it a second time.

About ten minutes later, the hanger on my middle rod dropped back about three inches. Once again there was no further indication, so I tightened up the line, and left that rod too. I must admit that I was a little worried that the presentation on these two rods might now be less than perfect, and I made up my mind to re-cast them both at about midday. In fact, I very nearly re-casted them both straight away, but my decision to leave them was to prove to be a good one.

At ten to eleven that morning I heard the delkim to my left once again, but this time, when I reached the rod the line was out of the clip and the spool was ticking slowly.

I picked up the rod and at first I felt no resistance, but after I retrieved a couple of yards or so of line, I soon came into contact with the fish. It had found the sanctuary of some weed, and I bent the rod into it quite firmly, to try to force it out. I didn`t want to put too much pressure on, and pull the hook out, but I had to get the fish moving. Nothing happened at first, and I feared the worst, but after thirty seconds or so I felt the fish kick.

What a relief!

Thirty seconds doesn`t sound long as I write it here, but it seemed like an eternity to me, and I was starting to think that it was gone. I then just kept steady pressure on the fish, and let it kick itself free. Despite the weed that was between myself and the fish, I managed to bring it towards me relatively easily. The lead had discharged on the take, so most of the time the fish was on the surface, which helped a lot. A short time later the carp was only about five yards out and I could see that it was a decent mirror, not enormous, but a good start all the same. I thought that I`d be able to net it quite easily, but the carp had other ideas and it powered away from me for about fifteen to twenty yards. This happened on a couple more occasions, and there was a large ball of weed on the end of the lead-core which was making it difficult for me to get a direct pull on the fish. The carp was tired now though, and the next time that I brought it towards me, I was able to lift the net around it.

Whenever you land a carp there is always that feeling of euphoria, but after so long without one, and after my disappointing time at Contre, my success tasted even sweeter.

I staked the net to the bank with a bank-stick, and started to get the mat, scales, camera etc. ready, and as I was doing this, one of the French anglers came walking towards me.

'Have you caught a fish?' he asked.

'Yes a mirror' I told him, and I showed him the carp in the net. He offered to take some photos for me, so I handed him my camera, and thanked him.

The carp weighed just short of 33 lbs. at 32 lbs.15 oz. and the photos turned out quite well.

After returning the fish to the lake, I tied some more tigernuts onto the rig, and casted it back out to the same position as before. I also re-casted my middle rod, on which I`d had the drop-back earlier that morning, although to be honest, I think that it had been perfectly fine all along. I certainly couldn`t see anything wrong with the rig or the hook-bait when I retrieved it.

I put out about thirty more boilies with a throwing stick, around each hook-bait, and then started to make some dinner. It was sweet and sour chicken with rice, followed by fresh oranges, and I was looking forward to it.

At about three o`clock, I was part-way through sticking out some more boilies when Benoit arrived to see me. He had promised to go to get a permit for me for the lake at Argoeuves, the lake that we had found about two weeks earlier, and that would involve him catching a bus to Amiens, and back again. I would have gone myself, but I didn`t know the way to the shop and I couldn`t leave my tackle.

'It`s a pity that Clément isn`t here at the moment' I said, 'because he could have watched my tackle, while I drove you there in my car. That would have been much easier.'

Then Benoit had an idea. His father had that day off work, so Benoit rang him to ask if he would watch my tackle for an hour, while we were away. His father agreed, and about twenty minutes later he arrived at the lake, and Benoit and I were on our way to Amiens.

The journey through Amiens was very complicated, and I would never have found it by myself, but by following Benoit`s directions, we were soon parked just a few yards away from the tabac, which we had been told sold the permits. Unfortunately there was a problem.

The tabac was closed, and it looked as though it was closed permanently.

We were not to be defeated so easily however, and Benoit looked up the fishery website on his phone, and it mentioned a café which also sold permits, and as it wasn`t far away, we decided to leave the car and walk there. About fifteen minutes later we arrived at the café, and we asked the proprietor about a 'carte de Peche'. Unfortunately he said that he didn`t know anything about it, and that they certainly didn`t sell them there.

We were really struggling, and I told Benoit that we needed to speak to someone connected with the fishery, to get some up to date information. So Benoit went back to his phone and onto the fishery website again, and he looked for some phone numbers of people that he could talk to. He found four numbers and started dialling. There was no reply to the first three numbers that he called, and we were starting to give up hope, but when he dialled the last number, which was for the secretary of the fishery, a woman answered. She said that her husband was not in unfortunately, but when Benoit explained what we wanted, she told him that the permits could be bought from a shop called 'Terres & Eaux', which was about ten kilometres from Amiens. It was now six o'clock in the evening, but she said that the shop was open until 7.30 pm, so he thanked her for her help, and we walked back to the car. We found the shop with no trouble at all, and a few minutes later I parted with 89 euros, and I was given my permit for Argoeuves in exchange. I was delighted, and I made up my mind to fish there on my next trip to France in August.

We headed back to Loeuilly, but not before I bought a few bottles of beer as a thank you to Benoit and his father for all of their help.

I re-casted my rods at half past seven that night, put fifty or so boilies around each one and then sat down for a rest.

I woke early the next morning, to find everything exactly as I'd left it the night before. I'd barely heard anything during the night, which was very disappointing.

At a quarter to eight, I had decided to re-cast the rods and I was sitting in my bivvy tying up a rig, when the delkim on my middle rod started to make that lovely warbling sound. When I reached the rod, the hanger was tight to the butt, but I soon discovered that the fish was in weed. I bent the rod into the fish, to try to pull it clear, but nothing was moving and the fish was stuck solid. I tried again, but that obviously wasn't working, so I slackened off the clutch, put the rod back on the rest, and went back to my bivvy to wait. It didn't take long, and a couple of minutes later the delkim started to shriek again as line was taken from the reel. I tightened up the clutch and bent the rod into the fish again, and at first I thought that it might be ok as I was able to gain a little line, but then everything became solid. Once again I slackened off the clutch and put the rod back on the rest, but now I was beginning to fear the worst.

While I was waiting, I re-casted my left-hand rod, put about thirty boilies around the hook-bait with a throwing stick, and then went back to deal with my middle rod. Since I`d put the rod down for the second time, I hadn`t heard a sound from that delkim, so I was sure that the fish had gone and it was just a case of retrieving the rig. Unbelievably, when I lifted the rod and put some pressure on, I felt the fish move and I was able to bring it towards me. At twenty past eight, more than half an hour after I`d first hooked it, I was able to net the carp. It wasn`t particularly big, but I was delighted to have landed it after all had seemed lost.

I rang Benoit but got no reply, and the French angler on the point swim was asleep, so I decided to take the photos myself. The carp was a mirror of 25 lbs.10 oz., and I soon had the self-takes done and the fish returned safely to the lake.

I re-casted the rod and then put about thirty boilies around each hook-bait with a throwing stick. The rest of the morning was very busy as I had several visitors. First Benoit came, and he stayed for an hour or so, promising to return in the afternoon. He said that he had been asleep when I had tried to call him, and he had discovered a missed call from me when he woke, so he came to the lake straight away. Next Beloit's sister arrived with her new boyfriend. I had never met her boyfriend before, but he seemed like a very nice chap. Lastly Timothée came to see me and we talked for half an hour or so. I told him that I had caught just two mirrors so far and that I was surprised that I hadn`t caught any grass carp, because I had always caught grass carp when I had fished in this swim in the past.

Amazingly, just ten minutes after Timothée left, I hooked my third fish of the session, and a few minutes I landed a huge grass carp. Once it was in the net, it went ballistic, as grass carp often do, but I was confident that with the net being secured to the bank with a bank-stick, it would be perfectly safe. I got everything ready to weigh and photograph the fish, and then I walked to the point swim to ask for assistance. As we returned to my swim, the fish made a huge leap which caused the net to come free of the bank-stick, and the grass carp started to swim out into the lake, pulling the landing net behind it. Fortunately I was just able to grab the end of the handle before it disappeared out of sight, and I pulled the net and fish back towards me.

It was a magnificent fish, and at a weight of 29 lbs.14 oz. it was a personal best for me, for a grass carp. Thomas, the French angler who was helping me, took some excellent photos, and then we returned the fish safely to the lake.

The fish had taken an orange pop-up on my middle rod, so I tied on a similar hook-bait, and soon had it back out in position. I then put about thirty boilies around it with a throwing stick, and did the same for the other two rods.

The afternoon and early evening were very quiet, and I didn't see a single fish show, despite the wind dropping, which made fish spotting much easier. I re-casted my middle rod at eight o'clock with a pink pop-up this time, but I left the other two rods as they were. I was using tigernuts on both of these rods, and had been very happy with the casts that I'd made that morning, so I saw no need to disturb them. Because it had been so quiet during the last few hours, I decided to bait more heavily that evening, so I put out about seventy boilies and twenty tigernuts around two of my rods, and about fifty tigernuts and several balls of boilie paste around my right-hand rod. Hopefully that would help produce another fish for me, if not during the night, then probably in the morning.

The night was very quiet with not a breath of wind, but at two o'clock in the morning, I was woken by the delkim to my left, and I was soon standing there with the rod showing a healthy bend. The fish was in weed, but this time I was able to force it through the weed and into open water relatively easily, and a little while later I caught my first sight of the fish in the light of my head-torch. When I saw the fish I was a little worried because it looked like a grass carp, and a big one at that. Now I love catching grass carp, but they can be a nightmare in the net and on the bank, so trying to deal with one by myself in the dark was going to be very difficult. I would have to take the pictures straight away too, because I never sack grass carp, because I just don`t think that it`s safe. I have no worries at all about sacking carp, but grass carp are totally different, and they just get too stressed.

I managed to net the fish at the first attempt, and when I shone my head-torch into the net, I discovered that I had been completely wrong. It wasn`t a grass carp at all, it was a mirror. The carp was very long and thin, which is why I`d mistaken it for a grass carp .The fish was so long in fact, that had it been the more usual more rounded shape that most mirrors are, then it would probably have weighed well in excess of forty pounds, but because it was so thin, it stopped the scales at just 30 lbs.13 oz. I was happy enough with my fourth fish of the session however, and I put it into a sack which I carefully placed in the deep margin, ready for Benoit to take some photos in the morning.

I didn`t re-cast the rod because I couldn`t see my far-bank markers in the dark and it would be very difficult for me to cast accurately to the small clear area which was surrounded by weed. I would re-cast it at first light, which was now only about three hours away.

At ten to seven that morning, when I heard one of my delkims shriek, I was surprised to find that it was my right-hand rod, the first take that I`d had on that rod all session.

The bobbin had dropped right back to the ground, and when I took up the slack line, I was pleased to feel a fish kick, and I was able to bring the fish towards me very easily. Now I know that there was far less weed in front of this rod, but it still shouldn't have been quite so easy, so I was beginning to have my doubts about what I'd hooked. Sure enough, just a short time later my fears were realised, when I lifted the net around a bream.

Not really what I wanted at that time in the morning.

I unhooked and returned the bream, and walked back to my bivvy, without bothering to re-cast the rod. I had only been back in my bivvy about five minutes, when I heard another of my delkims. It was my middle rod this time and there was no doubt about the culprit, because I could see a carp on the surface as soon as I made contact. I brought the carp through the weed quite easily, and then it started to kite to the left. Fortunately I hadn't re-casted either of the other rods, so there were no other lines in the water to worry about, and it was a simple matter of just walking along the bank to my left, where I was able to net it. It was only a small fish, but I was delighted with it because it was a common, which are very rare in this lake. I weighed the carp at 12 lbs.13 oz. and then I texted Benoit to let him know that there were two carp waiting to have their photographs taken.

I re-casted all three rods, and put some more bait out, before I had something to eat while waiting for Benoit. It was hot and sunny with only a light wind, and although it was still early, I sat there sweltering in the heat. Fortunately I didn't have to wait long, and Benoit soon arrived to help me with the photos. It was a good job that Benoit was there to help, because the mirror was very lively on the mat, after having been sacked for a few hours. If it was a boxing match, I think the ref would have stopped the fight to save me from further punishment, as the carp repeatedly slapped me around the face with its tail, but we final got the photos taken and the fish were both returned safely.

It remained hot for most of the day, but there was a moderate north-westerly wind which made the high temperature more bearable. As I sticked out some more boilies that afternoon, I was happy with the five fish that I`d caught, but thought to myself that one more would round the session off nicely. There were a lot of canoeists on the lake, enjoying themselves in the warm sunshine. They were making a lot of noise and splashing about, but I`m sure that the carp are used to this, because there are canoeists on the lake on most days at this time of the year, and I don`t think it bothers them. None of the canoeists came close enough to disturb my lines, so it didn`t upset me at all. I was just watching two young girls that had fallen out of their canoe into the water, and two others were helping them to get back in, when I heard one of my delkims scream. It was my left-hand rod on which I was using a white pop-up, and I was soon playing what seemed to be a big carp. The fish had a lot of power and it took quite some time for me to bring it towards me, but when I got the fish to about ten or twelve yards from the bank, it really began to fight. I would slowly gain a couple of yards of line, only for the carp to power away from me and take the line that I`d gained back again, and with interest. This went on for ten or fifteen minutes, during which time I wasn`t able to get the fish to the surface or to bring it any closer, so I still hadn`t even seen it, and my estimate of its size was going up and up.

Was this my first forty of the session?

As I fought the fish, a passer-by had stopped to see what was going on, and he watched in fascination as I battled what was obviously a very big fish. I couldn`t understand why the fish hadn't tired by now, after what had been a tremendous fight. I wasn't sure who was winning this battle, because if the fish wasn't tired, then I knew that I certainly was.

Eventually I was able to force the carp to the surface, and what I saw amazed me. The fish was definitely not a forty, in fact it was a mid-twenty at best, but why had it given me so much trouble. It had fought much harder than any of the bigger fish that I'd caught that week.

I placed the carp into the sling and hoisted it onto the scales, where it weighed 25 lbs.12 oz, which the man who'd been watching me said was 'énorme'. He took a few photos for me but he was obviously not used to using a camera. He must have touched just about every button on the camera, but fortunately with a little work on my computer when I got home, I managed to salvage a couple of decent pictures.

I re-casted the rod, using a washed-out pink pop-up this time, and put out a further thirty boilies around it. That was the last of my bait, so that would have to do for the session, but judging by the amount of digested bait that the last carp had left on the mat, the bait was definitely working.

At half past six I had another take on the left-hand rod once again, but the fish had taken a washed-out pink pop-up this time. I brought the fish towards me quite easily and I had my suspicions that this might be another grass carp. Very often they allow themselves to be brought towards the bank relatively easily, but then they go ballistic under the rod- tip, and in the net too of course. As I brought the fish towards me I could see that it was indeed a grass carp, and I couldn't believe my luck when I was able to slide it across the surface to the waiting net, at the first attempt. I should have known better however, because when it was about a foot away from the net, it turned with a flurry of spray and powered away from me again. This was repeated a dozen times if not more, before I was finally able to lift the net around it. I secured the net to the bank with a bank-stick, and then I prepared the scales, sling, mat etc. There were a couple of anglers fishing just up the bank from me who had arrived earlier in the day, and one of them offered to take the photos for me. His help was very much appreciated because grass carp can be absolute idiots on the bank sometimes. In this case however, once on the mat, the grass carp behaved impeccably, and we were able to weigh it and take some photos without any trouble at all. The grass carp weighed 19 lbs.5 oz. and was a lovely looking fish, which we were pleased to see swim strongly away, when we released it back into the lake.

At twenty past nine that evening, I had yet another take on my left-hand rod, and I soon found myself playing another grass carp. They certainly seemed to like those washed-out pink pop-ups. This fish was a bit bigger than the last, but despite that, I was able to net it without too much trouble, but then all hell broke loose.

The grass carp didn`t like being in the net at all, and it leapt into the side of the net, to try to get out. It must have done this at least half a dozen times, until it smashed right through the mesh and swam out the other side, back into the lake. It was still attached to my line, so I quickly grabbed the rod and pulled the fish back towards me. There was no point trying to get it back into that net though, because there was now a large hole in it, so I ran to get the other landing net, and netted it with that. I then cut the line just above the lead-core, and fixed the net to the bank with a bank-stick. I then went to ask my friends in the next swim for some help, and between us we were able to weigh the fish and take some photos.

This one weighed 26 lbs. exactly and was a superb fish, but at what cost. I already had a small hole in one landing net, which had been caused by the first grass carp that I'd caught, but now my other net was totally ruined. That was two new nets that I was going to have to buy, when I got back to England.

I decided not to re-cast my left-hand rod, because I really didn't want to catch any more grass carp. With only one usable net, and that with a small hole in it, I just didn't think that my tackle could stand catching another. I was leaving the next morning and wanted to start packing up early, so catching more fish wouldn't really help. I did leave my other two rods in position, but I hadn't had a take on either of those for some time. I'd caught eight fish this session, and that was plenty enough for me, so I grabbed a quick snack and went to bed for some much needed sleep.

I caught nothing overnight, which was a relief really, and when I woke at six o'clock the next morning, I reeled in the rods and started to pack up.

CHAPTER TEN - ALBERT

Albert is a lake that I had fished quite often in the past, and I had been very successful there, but it was my first session at the lake this year, so I was really looking forward to it. My friend Corentin had managed to get a couple of days off work, and he would be fishing with me, so that made it all the better. It is a lake of about twenty acres, with an average depth of about five feet, and contains several small islands. There are some gravelly areas, which most of the local anglers tend to fish to, but I have preferred to fish on the more silty areas in the past, with some success. Because there is very little weed present and very few snags, it is an ideal lake to fish with a light running lead on a slack fluorocarbon main-line, and this is the way that I have always approached it. I have caught carp there to just over forty pounds, but they are gradually increasing in size and the future of the lake looks bright.

For once there weren`t any roads closed or diversions on my way down to Dover, so I arrived more than an hour and a half before my check-in time. I was fortunate to get on an earlier ferry, and just before six o`clock on Friday morning I arrived at Albert. It was still dark, but by the time that I`d barrowed my kit to the swim, it was just getting light, and I could see what I was doing.

I chose to fish on the first platform, a swim that I`d fished several times in the past, and quite successfully. I was just setting up my first rod, when I looked up and saw Corentin standing next to me. I hadn`t heard him arrive, so I nearly jumped out of my skin, but we both laughed and then chatted for a while.

Having fished this swim before, I had a good idea where to place my hook-baits, so I soon had the rods clipped-up to the correct distances and I baited three of the four spots heavily with just boilies. My fourth rod was to be fished in the right-hand margin, and I baited this spot differently, using hemp, pellets, chopped tigers and chopped boilies.

The afternoon was extremely hot and the temperature soared to well over thirty degrees. Understandably, neither Corentin nor myself caught any carp in those conditions, but Corentin did manage to catch one small grass carp, and we both hoped that the evening would bring us more success, as the temperature dropped.

The wind dropped completely that evening but it remained very warm, and neither of us saw any signs of carp in our swims at all. I was very tired after the journey to France the previous night, so by nine o`clock I was fast asleep in my bivvy. I was expecting some action during the night, but when I woke at about three o`clock the next morning I was very disappointed that I hadn`t heard a single bleep from my delkims, and wondered what was wrong. I didn`t stop to think about it too long however, and soon turned over and went back to sleep.

I was woken at just after five o`clock by a screaming delkim. It was on the rod that I`d casted towards the willow, and when I reached the rod the delkim was still screaming and the fish was taking line despite the clutch on my reel being set quite tight. The carp gave me a tremendous fight, especially when I brought it close to the net. I had caught a glimpse of the fish in the light of my head-torch, and I saw that it was a common of about twenty pounds, but it fought like a fish of twice its size. Eventually I was able to land it and fixed the net to the platform with a bank-stick so that it couldn`t escape, before starting to prepare everything to weight the fish and take the photos. Although Corentin was only in the next swim, he was asleep, so I decided not to disturb him for what was not a particularly big fish, and take the photos myself. I didn`t get the chance however, because while I was setting up the camera, I had another take. This fish fought even harder than the first, and it must have taken at least twenty minutes, but eventually I was able to lift the net around another common. This fish looked a bit bigger than the first, and I guessed that it was probably a mid-twenty.

I now had carp in both of my landing nets, and if I had another take I`d be in a bit of trouble, so I went to wake Corentin to help me. It was just getting light now, so that would make it much easier to take the photos.

When I lifted the first net out of the water, I was amazed to see that there was a mirror carp inside. I`d only seen the fish in the light of my head-torch, while it was still in the water, but I`d been convinced that it was a common. The mirror weighed just short of twenty pounds at 19 lbs.8 oz. and slapped me in the face a couple of times with its tail as I was trying to lift it for the camera, just to get its own back.

The second carp was a common as I`d thought, and was a beautiful fish which weighed 26 lbs.14 oz.

After we`d returned the fish, I re-casted both rods, put a few boilies over the top with a catapult, and then we both went back to our bivvies to get some more sleep. It was now almost half past seven, but I wasn`t able to rest for long, because at a quarter to eight I had my third take of the morning.

I could tell straight away that this was a much bigger fish than the other two, and called out to Corentin to come to help me. Unfortunately Corentin was fast asleep and didn`t hear me, so when I called a second time and still got no response, I gave up and concentrated on playing what seemed to be a very big fish. A couple of minutes later my friend Pierre-Jean appeared by my side. He had been fishing in a swim on the other side of the lake and had seen me playing the fish, so he`d come to help. He tried to shake hands with me when he arrived, which was quite difficult for me, because I had one hand holding the rod and the other holding the reel handle, so we both laughed and I went back to playing the fish. When I slid the carp over the net-cord, I could see that it was a big mirror, and from the depth of it I realised that it must be very close to forty pounds. I hoisted it onto the scales and unfortunately the dial stopped just short of the magic forty pounds mark, but at 38 lbs.4 oz. it was still a fantastic fish.

Just a few hours before I hadn`t heard a bleep from my alarms and I was worrying that it just wasn`t happening, but now I`d caught three carp in no time at all, including a 38,

How things can change.

I re-casted the rod, but with a pop-up this time, despite the fact that the last three takes had been to bottom-baits. The only reason that I changed it was that the critically-balanced bottom-baits that I`d just taken that last fish on were damaged, and I already had a pop-up tied up on a new rig. Yes I know it was a bit lazy of me, but I`d definitely have critically-balanced bottom-baits on the rig when I casted it out the next evening. I catapulted another thirty or so boilies around each spot, and then I had a bite to eat. The sun was shining down out of a cloudless blue sky, and it was already quite hot. It was going to be another scorcher, and I didn`t expect any more action until it cooled down again in the evening, but you never know.

At just after five o`clock that afternoon I started to tie up my rigs and pva bags that I was going to use that evening, and I had just finished doing that when I had a screaming take on my second rod. It was totally unexpected because I`d seen no carp activity whatsoever, and it was still very hot indeed. Corentin heard my delkim and was soon standing by my side with the net. As I played the carp we realised that it was another big fish, and when I brought it to the surface and saw the length of it, I was sure that I'd hooked my first forty of the session. It took quite some time because it was a very strong fish, but ten or fifteen minutes after I'd first hooked it, Corentin had the carp in the net. He parted the mesh to have a look at the carp, and he agreed with me that it looked at least forty pounds. When I put the fish on the mat however, I wasn't quite so sure. It was a very long fish, but it wasn't very deep, and on the scales it weighed just 34 lbs.2 oz. The weight was a little disappointing, but it was still a beautiful fish, and I caught it at a time when I hadn't expected to catch anything, so it was a bonus really.

The carp had taken a washed-out pink pop-up, just like some of those grass carp that I'd caught at Loeuilly the previous month, and I wondered if the method would work at Argoeuves, where I was going on Monday. I would certainly give it a try.

I re-casted all of my rods just after seven o'clock that evening, Three of them with double bottom-baits, and my fourth rod, which was being fished in the near margin, with a snowman. I then baited three of the spots heavily with just boilies, and the near spot with chopped boilies, chopped tigers, pellets and hemp. I was very happy with all four rods and was expecting some more action, but thought that I would have a better chance later in the night, or perhaps even in the early morning when it was a little cooler, because it was still very hot.

The night was very quiet indeed. I did hear three or four single bleeps from my left-hand delkim, which I assumed were caused by crayfish, but I heard nothing at all from the other three, and I woke at first light the next morning without adding any more carp to my tally.

I could see that Corentin was awake, so I walked to his swim to see if he`d fared any better. Unfortunately Corentin hadn`t caught any carp that night either, which was very disappointing, and the only reason that we could think of to explain our lack of action, was the very hot weather.

When I retrieved my left-hand rod I discovered that the hook-bait had been partly eaten away, and it seemed that I had been right when I assumed that the single bleeps that I`d heard the previous night, were caused by crayfish. The other three hook-baits were all in perfect condition, and I'd heard nothing from the other delkims, so it seemed that the crayfish were only present in the left-hand side of my swim.

It was warm and sunny again at first, but as the day wore on more and more clouds appeared, and at half past eleven it started to rain. It then rained quite heavily for the rest of the day, which made it quite uncomfortable, but we hoped that it might improve the fishing a little. There were still no signs of any carp in our swims, so after I re-casted the rods at about half past five, I decided to bait very heavily with boilies. Nothing was happening, so I didn`t think that I had anything to lose by doing this, and I hoped that it just might provoke a fish or two into feeding. All the rods were in position and all the spots were baited by about six o`clock, so I went back to my bivvy to wait.

Just ten minutes later I had a take on my left-hand rod. I had very little difficulty with the fish, and a couple of minutes later I had a mid-twenty mirror in the net.

Perhaps the heavy baiting was starting to work.

After so long without a fish, it was quite a relief. We weighed the carp, which was 26 lbs.10 oz. and Corentin took the photos.

The hook-bait that I`d caught the fish on didn`t look quite right, so I changed it for a new one, and re-casted the rod. I was just waiting for the line to sink, and still had the rod in my hands, when I had a take on my second rod. I quickly put the first rod down, picked up the second rod, and started to play another carp. I called for Corentin for help, because I was worried that the carp would swim across my other line, which I hadn`t had time to sink properly. Corentin soon moved that rod for me, and I was then able to play the fish without any worries, and shortly afterwards he lifted the net around another mirror of about the same size as the last. It actually weighed 27 lbs.6 oz. and after weighing it and taking the photos, we returned it to the lake and watched it swim away strongly.

I had to tie up a new rig before I could re-cast, because I had mistakenly cut the hook-link. Before I take the fish out of the water, to put it onto the mat, I usually cut the main-line just above the rig (or just above the leader, if I`m using one). This means that I can move the rod well out of the way, so it makes everything much easier, and safer for the fish. This time however, I managed to cut the hook-link instead of the main-line, and ruined the rig.

What a plonker!

I had hoped that introducing a lot of bait might make something happen, but two fish in less than half an hour was beyond my wildest dreams, especially after24 hours without one.

I was just about to go to bed, just after dark, when I heard a series of bleeps from one of my delkims. I hurried to the rods, but was surprised to see that although the delkim was bleeping, the hanger was not moving, and there was no movement of the line at all.

'It must be the battery' I thought, so I changed it for a new one, but that still didn`t cure the problem. Corentin and I tried everything we knew, and even tried a third battery, but we couldn`t find an answer. Fortunately I carry a spare delkim with me, so I swapped the faulty one for my spare, which worked perfectly. The only problem with my spare delkim is that it is an older type, and not a 'TXI', and it doesn`t work on my remote, so I turned up the volume to maximum and hoped that I`d hear it if I had a take during the night. The rod wasn`t far away from the bivvy, so although I`m quite a heavy sleeper, I thought that it should wake me. I wasn`t sure though, and I lay awake for some time worrying about it.

As it happened, I needn`t have worried at all, because I didn`t hear a single bleep from any of my alarms all night long. I was really surprised because the conditions seemed perfect to me, but that just goes to show you how much I know!

Monday morning was dry at first, but it soon clouded over and started raining heavily, so both myself and all my tackle got absolutely soaked as I barrowed it to the car.

Lovely!

CHAPTER ELEVEN – ARGOEUVES

I arrived at Argoeuves for my first ever session there, just after half past eleven in the morning, and I was the only one there. I had a walk around, and decided on a swim mid-way along the far bank. I thought that it looked very good, but I would have to use my barrow to get all of my gear to the swim, because there was a barrier preventing access by cars to that area. I nearly chose a swim on the near bank, where I would have been able to drive to the swim, but eventually decided on the far bank.

That was a decision that I would regret.

It had stopped raining when I arrived, but there were still a lot of dark clouds around, so I took the bivvy to the swim first, and set it up. I then went back to my car to get the first barrow-load of tackle. The bed-chair and sleeping bag were now in my bivvy in the dry, which was a big plus. I decided to go back to the car for the rods and the rest of my tackle, before putting the over-wrap onto my bivvy, so I put it by the door and walked back to the car. On the way I saw two men walking towards me and I stopped to say 'Bonjour', before carrying on walking to the car. As I loaded my barrow, another angler arrived, and we talked for a minute or so. He was called Claude and he had brought his son fishing to the lake.

There was a large black cloud bearing down on us, so we wished each other 'Bonne Peche' and I pushed the barrow back to my swim as fast as I could. Unfortunately I wasn't fast enough, because the heavens opened and I was soaked for the second time that day. When I reached my bivvy, the rain was absolutely torrential, so I leapt inside and zipped shut the door. There was water everywhere as it dripped off me onto the bivvy floor, and mud off my boots too, but it was still better than being out there in the rain.

After half an hour or so the rain eased a little, so I unzipped the door and went outside to put the over-wrap on the bivvy, and then I got a horrible surprise.

My over-wrap was gone!

I hadn't noticed that it was missing when I got back to the swim, because I was more interested in getting out of the rain. I couldn't believe it at first, and I looked all around the bivvy, and even inside, but it was definitely gone. Someone must have stolen it while I was getting the rest of my tackle from the car, and I was convinced that it was the two men that I had spoken to. I couldn't prove it however, and I didn't even know their names, so there was nothing that I could do about it.

I was absolutely devastated.

What a start to my fishing on the new lake.

I had bought the over-wrap when I had bought my latest bivvy, just over a year before, and the wrap had cost £250, but it wasn't just the money. The over-wrap made the bivvy double-skinned, so it stopped any condensation. It also created a porch section in the front, which gave me an area to place buckets, boots etc. and this porch section stopped ant rain from blowing into the the bivvy. Without it, the rain would be blown in the front of the bivvy by the strong wind, and either the bivvy would get soaked, or I would have to zip the door shut during the windy rainy weather, which looked like lasting for some time. In warm sunny weather it wouldn't have been much of a problem, but with the torrential rain and strong winds that I was enduring here, it looked like I was going to have a very uncomfortable next three days.

The other thing that worried me was the fear that the thieves might return during the night. I am much too old to start fighting off thieves, but I'd just have to hope that they didn't come back. At least there were some other anglers at the lake now. Claude was on the opposite bank, and two anglers had just arrived on the east bank, so that made me feel a little bit safer.

The one consolation about the theft was that I was insured. There was a sporting goods extension on my home insurance that I had paid for, which covered my fishing tackle away from the house, and even abroad, so I rang my wife Anita, to ask her to report the loss to the insurance company.

A few minutes later Anita rang me back to tell me that there was a problem with the claim, and that someone from the insurance company would ring me on my mobile within the hour, to explain it to me. Sure enough, about fifteen minutes later my phone rang, and it was a girl from the insurance company. She told me that although my fishing tackle was insured, because I had paid extra for that cover, they didn't class a bivvy as fishing tackle. She said that it was a tent and that was classed as camping equipment, which wasn't covered under my policy. Because the over-wrap was part of this 'tent', it was not insured. All of those years of paying the premiums without a claim, and when something does happen, I'm not insured.

Don't you just love insurance companies!

All afternoon and evening there were very heavy showers most of the time, and I had to keep sheltering inside my bivvy, so setting-up took hours. I finally did find three spots that I was happy with, but by the time that these were all baited and I'd casted the hook-baits into position, it was half past eight and only an hour before dark.

While I'd been searching for suitable spots with my marker rod, I'd discovered that the lake was quite deep, with an average depth of about 14 or 15 feet, and even just a couple of yards from the margin it was at least eight feet deep. I've caught carp from those sorts of depths many times in the past of course, but I must admit that I'm much happier fishing in shallower water.

There was virtually no weed present at all, and the lake-bed was mainly smooth firm silt, which would normally have been perfect for me to fish with light running leads on a slack fluorocarbon main-line, but the very strong winds made that impossible, so I opted for 2½ oz. swivel leads in a lead-clip., and tight lines with heavy bobbins. The wind was howling across the lake towards me at forty or fifty miles per hour, with some gusts a lot stronger, and it really was quite unpleasant.

I fished with two rods at about 35 yards range, which I baited very heavily with boilies, and the third rod was casted about seven or eight feet from the left-hand margin. That one was baited with boilies too, but also with hemp, pellets and chopped tigers.

I must admit that I wasn't in the best of moods, and found it difficult to concentrate on my fishing. With the theft and the atrocious weather, I suppose that was understandable, but everything that I did, just seemed like hard work. Even my casting seemed difficult, and two out of the three rods needed a second cast to get it right. I know that there was a strong wind, which didn't help, but a thirty-five yard cast really isn't that difficult.

It was dark at half past nine that evening, and as I lay on my bed-chair listening to the rain beating down on the bivvy roof, I realised that I'd left my carp sacks in the car. If I did catch a carp, then I'd have to walk around the lake to the car to get them. That wouldn't be much fun in the rain. On the other hand, perhaps I wouldn't catch anything that night, and then I wouldn't have to bother. As the rain kept pouring down, I started to hope that I wouldn't catch.

Now that's not a good frame of mind to be in when you're fishing.

Because of my fears that the thieves would return in the night, I'd taken several precautions. I put everything that I could inside the bivvy, and set up several booby-traps. There were bungee ropes between the trees, and branches with thorns, and also several black buckets strategically placed, so if the thieves did return, I would definitely hear them. I also had a mallet next to my bed-chair, although what I was going to do with it, I'm not quite sure.

I doubted that these precautions were really necessary because I was sure that the thieves would have been tucked up at home warm and dry, rather than be out on such a foul night.

It was mild, but there was a very strong westerly wind and heavy rain , so I slept with the door zipped shut. I heard a couple of single bleeps from my alarms just after dark, but nothing after that, and I soon drifted off to sleep.

I was woken at half past eleven by a screaming delkim. It was my right-hand rod and I soon realised that it was a big fish. In the strong wind it was difficult to tell exactly what was happening, but I had to fight for every inch of line that I gained. It took a long time before I was able to bring the fish anywhere near me, and I could tell by the bend in the rod that this could be something very special. I then had a horrible thought –

'I hope that it isn't a catfish.'

I had been told that there were some catfish in the lake, and it was certainly a very strong fish. Shortly afterwards however, I breathed a big sigh of relief when I saw the fish near the surface for the first time, and it was definitely a carp. I tried to slide the landing net towards the water and to my horror I realised that the mesh of the net was tangled around the adjusting screw on the bank-stick. I always place a bank-stick on the ground next to each rod, and I use it to stake the net to the ground after I've landed a fish. That then gives me time to arrange mat, scales, water, camera etc. ready to weigh and photograph the fish, while it rests safely in the bottom of the net in the margin. I have done this for many years and have never had a problem before. I tried several times to untangle the net from the screw, which was very difficult because I was trying to play a big fish at the same time. Try as I may, I just couldn't untangle it, so I unscrewed the adjusting screw from the bank-stick, and I was then able to free the net. As I concentrated once again on playing the fish, I realised that it had gained about twenty feet of line while I was messing about with the net, and it took me quite some time to bring the fish back towards me again. When I did manage to get the fish close to me, the fight was still far from over, as the carp made good use of the deep water, and it took at least a further ten minutes for me to bring it back to the surface. I then watched the fish in the beam of light from my head-torch, as I slid it towards the waiting net, and lifted.

Instead of a heavy weight in the bottom of the net however, there was nothing there because I'd missed it. I could have sworn that I'd seen the fish come over the net cord, but somehow I'd messed it up. The fish was still on though, and the next time that I brought it towards me I made no mistake. I staked the net to the ground with the bank-stick that had given me so much trouble earlier on, and shone my head-torch into the net, where I saw a huge common staring back at me.

I was absolutely soaked once again, and the walk to the car to get my carp sacks didn't help matters, but it didn't matter to me at all. When I got back to my swim, I un-hooked the carp on the mat, and saw that the hook-hold was more than an inch back inside its mouth.

Absolutely nailed!

I then slid the fish into the sling and hoisted it onto the scales, where the dial flickered around forty for a while, before settling on 40 lbs.8 oz.

My first carp from Argoeuves, and it was a forty pound common!

That certainly made me feel better after the horrendous day that I'd had. I put the carp in a sack, and placed it in the margin, where it moved away from the bank strongly, and seemed quite happy. Hopefully the rain would stop in the morning, so that I could get some decent photos.

I didn't re-cast that rod. It gets very dark at night at Argoeuves, so I couldn't see my far-bank markers to re-cast accurately. I was soaking wet and just wanted to get back into the bivvy to dry off. I still had the other two rods in the water, and in any event, I was quite happy with the carp that I'd caught.

It would take quite some fish to top that.

Just before five o'clock the next morning I was woken by a take on my left-hand rod. I could hear bleeps from the delkim, and as I reached the rod I saw the hanger drop back a few inches. It was soon apparent that this carp wasn't as big as the first, but for a small fish it put up a spirited scrap. When I shone my head-torch into the net I saw a little mirror this time, which weighed just 6 lbs.4 oz. The rain had stopped at last, which made the weighing process much more comfortable, and I was able to return to my bivvy without getting soaked for a change. Once again I didn`t re-cast the rod, so now I had just the one rod fishing. It was only an hour or so until dawn, so I`d soon be able to take the photos of the big common, but I went back to bed to try to get a little more sleep first.

I hadn`t been back in the bivvy long when the middle rod was away. The fish put up a fantastic fight, rather like the big common, and I really struggled to bring it towards me. After about ten minutes or so, the carp began to kite to my right, towards the tree-line, and I was forced to apply a lot of pressure to stop it, but fortunately I just managed to turn it in time. It then stayed deep, about ten yards from the bank, and it took me ages to bring it to the surface, by which time my arm was really aching, which wasn`t what I wanted just before I had to hold a forty pound common for the camera. Eventually I did manage to bring it to the surface and I realised that it was another common, but if I thought that the fight was over, then I was wrong, because it dived down to the depths and it was another five minutes before I saw it again. This time however, I was able to slide it over the net-cord, and I punched the air with delight.

The carp weighed 31 lbs.6 oz. and because it still wasn`t quite light, I slipped it into a sack which I placed in the margin alongside the other common.

All of my rods were now out of the water, but at least that would give the swim a rest. About an hour after daybreak the light was just about perfect, and I thought that I`d catapult some more bait into the swim before doing the photos. While I was doing this, Claude arrived at my swim, and told me that he`d caught four fish, but they were all small grass carp, When I told him about the two carp in the sacks, he offered to take the photos for me, which was a big help. I must admit that I was a bit apprehensive about taking the pictures of the big common myself. It had been sacked for a few hours, so it was bound to be rather lively. Sure enough, the big common was a nightmare on the mat and I struggled to hold it properly, but with Claude`s help we did manage to get the photos done, although they could have been better. The other common was a little easier, fortunately.

Once Claude had returned to his swim, I finished putting the bait in and then sat down for a rest. I eventually re-casted the rods at about ten o`clock. The weather was a lot better, with warm sunshine and a clear blue sky, although there was still a strong westerly wind. That gave me a chance to get everything dry at last, which cheered me up no end.

Despite my problems of the previous day, as far as the fishing was concerned it couldn`t have been going much better. I had caught carp on all three rods, including two beautiful commons, and I thought that if this was what Argoeuves had to offer, then I`d definitely be back for some more.

At a quarter to one I was feeling a bit hungry so I started to make some dinner. I was making sweet and sour chicken with rice, and the saucepan had only been on the stove a couple of minutes when my right-hand delkim started singing its little tune. By the bend in the rod I could tell that this was another big fish. It stayed deep and made me work for every inch of line that I gained, just like the two commons that I`d caught in the night. This fish fought even harder however, and I just wasn`t able to bring it to the surface. It was in open water away from any snags, so I told myself to be patient, but that became more and more difficult as the minutes ticked by.

After more than half an hour of hard toil I finally caught my first glimpse of the fish, and I was surprised to see that it was a mirror, and a very big one at that. The carp still fought on, but as time went by it started to tire. By now another angler had come to watch me, and he asked if I wanted him to net it for me. I was glad of his help and he netted the fish perfectly. He seemed like a very nice chap and he offered to take the photos for me, but I didn`t know how good he was with a camera, so I decided to take them myself.

This was a huge fish and I didn`t want to take any chances.

After unhooking the carp on the mat, I put it into the sling and we hoisted it onto the scales. As I watched, I was delighted to see the dial fly past forty and finally settle on 47 lbs.13 oz. I told my friend that the weight was about 22 kilos and he was amazed.

After I`d taken half a dozen photos, I went to the camera to check, and I was disappointed to see that the shots were not correctly framed. The fish was so heavy that I must have moved slightly as I struggled to lift it. Lifting the beast was hard enough without having to do it twice.

I went back to try again, and fortunately the photos were fine this time. When I tried to lift the carp to take photos of its other side however, I was very tired and I just couldn`t lift it quite as high as I would have liked, but the pictures weren`t too bad.

Dinner was late, but I gladly accepted that after such a fantastic fish.

As the afternoon wore on the wind increased in strength, until it was very strong indeed. Several branches were blown off of nearby trees, which was a little disconcerting, but fortunately nothing landed on either me or my bivvy. It also became a little more cloudy, until at four o'clock it started to rain again. I zipped the bivvy door shut, and took the opportunity to have a short nap, and when I woke an hour or so later I was pleased to see that the rain had stopped.

It had been very quiet since I'd caught the big mirror, so that evening I baited heavily, hoping to encourage some fish to feed during the night. After dark the wind moderated slightly, but it was still quite strong. It was a very mild night and I had trouble sleeping. I lay there tossing and turning until about midnight, when I finally dropped off to sleep. I hadn't heard a single bleep from my delkims, which surprised me, but all that changed just before one o'clock the next morning, when I had a take on my right-hand rod.

As I came out of the bivvy I could see the hanger was tight to the rod butt and the clutch on my reel was ticking. I picked up the rod and came into contact with the fish, which came towards me very easily at first, so I suspected that it was either a very small carp, or perhaps a grass carp. When I brought it closer to me the fish fought a lot harder, but it was nothing like the battles that I'd had with the two commons and the big mirror, and I was soon able to lift the net around it. It was a mirror carp of 25 lbs.1 oz. and after I'd weighed it, I put it into a sack, which I placed in the margin.

I was just putting the mat away when I had another take, on my right-hand rod this time. It was a small mirror of just 8 lbs.14 oz. and although it tried hard, it wasn't much of a match for the strong tackle that I was using, and I soon had it in the net.

I didn't re-cast that rod because I was positioning the hook-bait near to the tree-line, and it was far too dangerous to try to make that cast in the dark. My other rod however was being fished in open water, so although I couldn't see my far-bank markers in the dark, it was perfectly safe, so I casted it out in the general direction of my spot. The cast was perfect for length of course, because I was using the line-clip on my reel, but the direction was guesswork really. It was worth a try though, and I doubted that it was too far away from where I wanted it.

That was the last action for the night, and I re-casted the rod at ten o`clock the next morning after taking the photos of the mirror.

It was warm with sunny periods, and the wind was a strong westerly, with occasional very strong gusts, which made the casting quite difficult. Despite the wind however, the first two casts were perfect. When I came to cast my third rod, the one that I`d re-casted during the night, I noticed from the angle of the line as it entered the water, that I`d positioned it at least ten yards to the left of my spot, so it wasn`t surprising that I hadn`t received any more takes to that rod. The sun was shining brightly into my eyes, so I was wearing a cap and sunglasses to help me to see, and as I was about to re-cast the rod, a strong gust of wind blew my cap off of my head, and into the lake.

I was devastated.

My lucky forest cap was lost!

To my amazement however, the cap didn`t sink as I had expected it to, but floated, and I watched the little red cap float along on the waves until it reached the bank, where I was able to pick it up.

What a stroke of luck.

I hadn`t lost my forest cap after all. It was very wet of course, but it would dry, so that was no problem at all.

I baited all three spots quite heavily again, and planned to bait just once more in mid-afternoon, which would use up all the rest of the bait that I had brought with me. It was my last day on the lake and I`d now decided that I would leave all the rods in position for the remainder of the session, unless they were disturbed by a fish of course.

I was using double critically-balanced bottom-baits on two of the rods, which was what I`d caught both of the forties on, so I was giving myself every chance. On my left-hand rod, on which I had only caught two small fish, I used a tigernut snowman, just to be different.

I saw no signs of any carp all day, and the lake was very busy. It was August, so a lot of the local people were on holiday, and quite a few of them had decided that it was a good idea to visit the lake. There were more carp fishermen than normal, but there were also several coarse fishermen too and a lot of picnickers, and people walking around. There were kids running about and generally quite a lot of noise, so it was no wonder that no carp were caught. I now remembered why I didn`t normally fish in France during August –

It`s just too busy!

It was my last night on the lake because I was returning to England in the morning, and although I hadn`t caught anything during the day, I was quite hopeful that the night would be different, when everything was quiet. If I didn`t catch any more fish, at least the mat and sling would be dry, which would make the journey home far more pleasant.

Wet mats and the aroma of fish is not nice in the car on a long journey!

It was dark at half past nine and once again the night was very mild. Although it was dark, I wasn`t tired, so I lay on my bed-chair reading. I was asleep by eleven o`clock, but I was woken at two o`clock the next morning by the sound of very heavy rain beating down on the bivvy roof once again. So much for my theory that if I didn`t catch on my last night, the mat would be dry for the journey home.

It looked like my last night would produce a wet mat and no carp.

And that`s the way it turned out. I took the rods out at half past six the next morning and started to pack up. The rain didn`t stop, and in fact it got heavier and heavier, so I got soaked once again when I barrowed my tackle back to the car.

Despite my early problems here, I`d had a fantastic session. I`d caught six fish in the three days that I`d spent at Argoeuves, including two forties and a thirty, so I was more than happy with that.

I`d already made up my mind to fish at Argoeuves again on my next trip to France in September, and if it was anywhere near as successful as this session, then I`d have a fantastic time. I would end my next trip with three days at Argoeuves, but first I`d spend four days at Contre. My last trip to the middle lake at Contre had been very disappointing. I caught just one small sturgeon and no carp at all. That was the first time that I had ever failed to catch a carp on the middle Lake and I was determined to make up for it.

CHAPTER TWELVE –
A RETURN TO THE MIDDLE LAKE

I arrived in Contre at about eight o`clock in the morning on Friday 11<sup>th</sup> September, and there were no other anglers there. The sun was shining out of a clear blue sky as I walked around the lake, and it looked like it was going to be a lovely day. There was no wind at all and I didn`t see any signs of fish, apart from a few bubbles near to the far bank, at the side of the peninsular swim, so I decided to fish there. I soon found some spots to fish – two close to the far bank on the left, and another about five yards from the far-bank near the front of the swim. Baiting up was easy, because I just walked around to the other side of the lake and threw it in by hand, which was not only very accurate, but it also caused very little disturbance. I didn`t use a lot of bait, just a few chopped tigernuts, a sprinkling of hemp and half a dozen boilies over each spot, so it didn`t take long.

I took my time organising my bivvy and all of my gear, and then I made myself something to eat and drink. I`d felt very tired after the long journey, but the food made me feel a little better, so I tied up the rigs ready to make my first cast of the session. I casted the left-hand rod first, with a washed-out pink pop-up, and it landed perfectly, just two feet short of the far bank. I then started to prepare the next rod, but as I was tying on the rig I heard a series of bleeps from my delkim.

'Surely not, I said to myself, 'It`s only been in the water about a minute!'.

It wasn`t a fish though. A couple of swans had been swimming past, and one of them must have touched the line. The second and third rods went in just as I had wanted, and I went back to the bivvy. It was quite hot now and I wasn`t expecting any action until it cooled down in the evening, so I thought that I`d take the opportunity to grab a couple of hours of sleep, while it was quiet. I had travelled overnight to France as I normally did. This meant that the journey through England was much easier, with far less traffic on the roads during the night, than if I`d travelled by day. That was good, but the downside was that I missed a night's sleep, and I was usually very tired during the first day of my sessions, so I lay down on my bed-chair and dropped off to sleep almost immediately.

I was woken just after three o`clock in the afternoon by my left-hand delkim. I was soon out of the bivvy and I picked up the rod quite quickly, but the fish had already found the sanctuary of a snag. I put a bit of pressure on, but the fish didn`t budge at all, so I slackened off the clutch and placed the rod back onto the delkim. Sometimes this works for me and sometimes it doesn`t, but this time I was lucky, and after only a couple of minutes I saw the indicator start to rise. I quickly lifted the rod and was back in contact with the fish, and to my relief I was able to pull it away from the far bank into open water. It was an extremely strong fish so it was a long time before I caught my first sight of the carp, as it broke the surface about ten yards in front of me. I realised that this was a very big fish and I started to worry about the hook-hold. I`d had to put a lot of pressure on the fish when it had been snagged early in the fight, and that couldn`t have helped the hook-hold at all. I tried to play it very carefully, but the carp started to kite to my right, towards one of my other lines, and I had to stop that at all costs. Fortunately I was able to turn the fish, and a few minutes later I lifted the net around it.

I looked into the net and saw a huge mirror, very dark in colour, and with several large scales on its flank. It was a gorgeous fish and looked to be at least forty pounds if not more. I noticed that the hook had caught in the top of the mesh, so I tried to unhook it in the net with my forceps. I struggled at first, but eventually the hook came free of the net and I breathed a big sigh of relief.

I couldn't believe it. After catching two forties on my last session at Argoeuves, it looked like I'd caught a forty here at Contre too, and the session was only a few hours old.

I staked the net to the bank with a bank-stick, and started to set up the weighing tripod, scales, camera etc. Eventually everything was ready – the sling had been zeroed on the scales, and I took a couple of test photos with the camera, which looked perfect. I walked back to the net and cut the main-line just above the rig, so that I could move the rod out of the way .I then removed the handle from the landing net, and rolled up the mesh, ready to lift the carp from the water. As I tried to lift it however, the bottom of the net caught on a branch in the margin, but I soon managed to free it and tried to lift the fish again. It was quite difficult because the fish was very heavy and the bank was steep, but with a bit of effort, I hauled the fish out of the water.

Then it all went wrong.

To my horror I heard the net rip, and almost as though it was in slow motion, I watched the carp slide through the large hole in the net, back into the water, and it was gone.

In all the years that I've been fishing, I'd never had this happen to me before. I'd had nets ripped in the past of course, but I'd never lost a fish because of it.

I'd caught a fantastic carp, and had returned it without knowing the weight and without a photo. It's hard to accurately guess the weight of that fish, but I really struggled to lift it and I'm sure that it was well in excess of forty pounds. I'm not certain what caused the net to rip either. It could have been damaged when the hook caught in the mesh. When I tried to remove the hook, I'd thought that it had just pulled free of the mesh, but of course it could have torn slightly. The net could also have been torn when it caught on that branch as I tried to lift it out of the water, and with the weight of that big fish, the rip would just get bigger and bigger. I'll never really know what had caused it, but I do know that I went from absolute elation when I caught that wonderful fish, to the depths of despair when I watched it slide back into the lake.

I always carry a spare mesh for my landing net with me, so when I'd fitted that, I re-casted two of my rods. It was just before seven o'clock that evening, and I used a pop-up on the left-hand rod and tigernuts on the middle rod, just as I had that afternoon, but this time I didn't add the little pva bags of mini halibut pellets. I'd had problems with both crayfish and rats on this lake in the past, so I decided to err on the side of caution.

At twenty to eight that evening, I was just tidying up the bivvy, when I had another take on my left-hand rod. When I picked up the rod I could feel the line grating on a branch, and I feared that this fish could be snagged just like the previous one, but this time I was able to guide the fish away from the bank, and into the safer open-water area. Once it was away from the snags I was able to gain line relatively easily, but then the carp started to kite to my left. There was a large overhanging bush in the left-hand near margin, and the carp headed straight for it, but I sank the rod-tip and applied a bit of pressure. This seemed to do the trick, and I was relieved to see the fish come past the bush. The rest of the fight took place within ten yards of me, and shortly afterwards the second carp of my session was inside of my net. It was another mirror which looked to be well over thirty pounds, but it seemed quite small compared to the last one.

Just how big was that other fish?

As you can imagine, I was quite nervous when I lifted the carp out of the water, but there was no problem this time, and I was soon holding it for the camera. It was quite a long fish, but without the depth of the last one and weighed 31 lbs.15 oz.

The hook-bait and rig both seemed fine, so I tied the rig back on and casted it back over towards the far bank once again. The wind had dropped completely now, and it was soon dark, so it wasn`t long before I was tucked up inside my sleeping bag, and knocking out the zzzz's.

Nothing happened during the night, and the next morning it was very quiet indeed, with no signs of any carp in the swim at all. Although conditions seemed to be perfect, and were definitely far better that the previous day, I wasn`t very hopeful about my chances of catching a carp. Sometimes you just get that feeling that it`s just not going to happen, and that`s how I was feeling now, but I had three hook-baits in the water, and would be quite happy to be proved wrong. I baited the far-bank spots again with chopped tigers, hemp and half a dozen boilies, and then I sat back in my chair and hoped for the best.

Just after one o`clock I had a take on my middle rod. The hanger lifted to the rod-butt, and then dropped to the ground as the lead discharged from the clip. As I picked up the rod I could feel a fish moving, but it didn`t feel like a carp, and I was able to bring it towards me far too easily. A short time afterwards I knew the reason why.

It was a tench.

I coudn't remember catching many tench in the past from Contre, and it probably weighed about a pound or so. I re-positioned the hook-bait once again near to the far bank, and then went back to the bivvy. Vincent arrived about half an hour later so I told him the story of my big fish and the ripped net, from the previous day. He sympathised and told me that the biggest carp that had ever been caught from this lake was a mirror of twenty kilos, which is 44 lbs, in real money, although that had been more than three years before, so it could be a lot bigger now. He said that the 20 kilo fish was not very long, but was very deep indeed, so it definitely wasn't the same fish that I'd caught. My fish was far better proportioned, was very dark and had several large scales on it's flank. Vincent asked me how big I thought that my fish was and I told him that I couldn't be sure, but I said that I had struggled to lift it, so I guessed that it was possibly 22 or 23 kilos, which is not far from the weight of my personal best. Maybe I'd catch it again someday, and then I'd know for sure.

In the afternoon the wind changed to a north-westerly direction and it rained heavily, so I was confined to the bivvy. I had bought a new overwrap, after my other one had been stolen at Argoeuves the previous month, so that had made me more comfortable, and I didn't need to zip the bivvy door closed to stay dry. I started to tie up some rigs, ready for a re-cast that evening, but at just after half past four, I was disturbed by a screaming delkim. It was my middle rod once again, and I soon found myself attached to another fish which I was able to steer away from the far-bank, without a great deal of difficulty. I slowly brought the fish towards me, and it was some time before I realised that it wasn't a carp, but another tench. This one was quite a bit bigger than the last, and probably weighed about four pounds. It had taken one of my cork-dust pop-up's, just like the last, so at least something was working. I often think that tench are a lot more difficult to catch than carp, because they tend to feed more carefully, but I'd managed to catch two tench, and no carp, that day. I still hadn't seen any signs of carp activity in my swim, so perhaps the reason that I wasn't catching carp was because they weren't there at the moment. If that was the case, then I hoped that they'd return soon.

I re-casted all of the rods at six o'clock that evening. On my left-hand rod I used a little yellow pop-up, and I used a snowman on my middle rod. I decided to re-position the third rod, and casted it about sixty yards towards the point. I used a washed-out pink pop-up on that rod, which had been my most successful presentation so far this session. I put half a dozen boilies around both of the far-bank rods, and about twenty around the third rod, and then I went back to the bivvy to make some dinner.

I don't know why, but for some reason I felt much more optimistic, despite not seeing any carp in the swim. All three casts had gone in perfectly, and I just felt that I was going to catch. It's strange when that happens. Of course if you see carp all over your swim it's understandable that you'd feel optimistic, but I hadn't seen anything. I just had that gut feeling that I would catch that evening.

About an hour or so later I was proved to be correct, when my right-hand delkim bleeped, and the hanger dropped back several inches. When I picked up the rod however, I was not pleased to see a small sturgeon leap clear of the water on the end of my line. Catching another sturgeon was definitely not on my to-do list, and this one weighed just 7 lbs.12 oz. The hook-bait had been damaged, so I tied on a new one, but I used a fluorescent yellow pop-up. Now fluorescent yellow is not a colour that I've got much confidence in, but I tried it anyway. I hoped that perhaps it would help me to avoid the sturgeon, but it may also help me to avoid the carp too.

Once again there was no further action during the night and I woke the next morning to find that it was cool and misty. As the mist cleared it started to rain, and as the day wore on the rain became heavier and heavier, until by early afternoon it was absolutely torrential, with a few claps of thunder too. The wind changed to a northerly direction, which blew the rain straight into the front of my bivvy, and I was forced to zip the door almost shut to stay dry. It was cold too, and I sat there wearing all my waterproof gear and a woolly hat, to stay warm. What I really wanted was an easterly wind, that would blow up the lake towards my swim, hopefully bringing some carp with it, but that didn`t look like it would happen anytime soon. I hadn`t seen any signs of carp what-so-ever, and I hadn`t heard a single bleep from my alarms, so it wasn`t looking good. The only activity in my swim was from half a dozen coots which were constantly diving, but none of them had picked up my hook-baits so far. If the coots didn`t want my baits, then what chance did I have from a carp?

I must admit that while the rain was at its heaviest, I was praying that I didn`t get a take, because I didn`t want to leave the shelter of my bivvy in that weather. Even with all of my wet-gear on, it wouldn`t have been very pleasant. I didn`t need to pray not to get a take however, because the swim looked so devoid of life, that the chances of a take seemed to be very unlikely indeed.

It finally stopped raining at about a quarter to five that evening, and the sun appeared briefly. I took the opportunity to hang my boilie bags on the tripod to get some air. These were the boilies that I was going to use at Argoeuves, and I had been worrying that the wet weather hadn`t allowed me to hang them out to dry since about lunch-time the previous day. The last thing that I wanted was for them to go off and be covered in mould. That certainly wouldn`t make them any more attractive to the carp.

I decided to try a plastic pop-up on my third rod for the coming night. The pop-up that I`d used on that rod the previous night had been almost totally eaten away by crayfish, and I hoped that a plastic bait would solve the problem. Unfortunately when I tested the rig, I discovered that it wasn`t buoyant enough to hold up a 360 rig. I tried it on a hinged stiff rig instead and it wasn`t buoyant enough for that rig either. I wasn`t in the mood to be beaten however, so I added a piece of rig foam, just under the plastic boilie, and tested it again. This time, I was pleased to see that it was slightly too buoyant, I cut small slivers off of the foam, a little bit at a time, and I was soon able to balance it perfectly. I sprayed the hook-bait with some white spice spray, that I had in my tackle box, to give it a bit of attraction, and I hoped that all of my effort would be rewarded. I realised that the spray would soon wash off of the plastic pop-up, but I hoped that perhaps the rig-foam would retain some of the flavour. I let the rod stand at the side of my bivvy for half an hour, to give the flavour every chance to soak into the foam, before I casted it out into position.

My friend Alexi arrived just as I was about to cast the rod, and he was quite surprised to see what I was using. We talked for a while and he nearly fell over laughing when I described the loss of the big mirror when my net ripped, and I couldn`t help but laugh with him. We talked for about an hour or so , before he left to get his evening meal. I re-casted the other two rods just before eight o`clock, both with pop-up`s wrapped in boilie mesh, and then I made myself something to eat. I didn`t put in any more bait, because I hadn`t received any indications at all during the day, so I presumed that most of the bait that I`d introduced in the morning, was still there. The coots had been diving, but they seemed to be feeding on the small amount of weed that was present, and I hadn`t seen any of them pick up a boilie. The crayfish didn`t seem to be a problem during the day, so I didn`t think that they`d cleared up the bait either. It was a totally different situation at night however, when the crayfish came out in force.

It was dark at a quarter to nine and the wind dropped completely, leaving the lake flat calm. This was ideal fish-spotting conditions, but unfortunately I didn`t see a single one. Whether they weren`t feeding, or they just weren`t in my part of the lake, I wasn`t sure, but it certainly didn`t fill me with confidence.

Not unexpectedly, I didn`t have any action during the night, but in the morning there was a light south-easterly wind, blowing up the lake towards my swim, which was better.

I re-casted my left-hand rod at half past nine, and the cast was perfect, exactly where I wanted it. I then went back to the bivvy to shelter from the rain, and as I watched, half a dozen coots swam towards my swim. I fired half a dozen boilies at them with my catapult, to try to scare them away, but they took no notice, and started diving. I then tried waving my landing net at them. That had often worked for me in the past, but it didn`t deter them this time. As I watched, one of the coots swam to where I`d just casted my hook-bait, where it dived, and a few seconds later my delkim sounded, and the hanger dropped back.

Great!

Rather than re-cast, I just tightened up the line to re-set the hanger, and left it. I didn`t think that the lead had ejected, and hoped that the rig was still presented well, after the coot

141

had dropped the hook-bait, but a couple of minutes later, my delkim sounded again as the hook-bait was picked up by another coot. I was tearing my hair out in frustration. I questioned their parentage, and then I explained to them in graphic detail exactly what I would have done to them, if only I'd had a gun, but they didn't seem to care.

At about a quarter past eleven, my middle rod was disturbed by the coots, and this time I decided to re-cast the rod, rather than to just leave it. I reeled in the rig and everything looked fine, but it started raining quite heavily, so I put the rod back onto the rest, and went back to shelter in my bivvy, to wait for the rain to stop. After about ten minutes, I heard a series of bleeps from my left-hand rod.

'Oh no, not again' I thought, but when I looked out of the bivvy, I could see that it wasn't a drop-back this time, and instead the hanger had risen to the rod-butt and stayed there. I picked up the rod and felt the satisfying weight of a carp. I was delighted and I leant into the fish, to try to ease it away from the far bank. The carp didn't want to come, but eventually the pressure told, and I had the fish in open water, and away from trouble. I hadn't yet re-casted my middle rod, so there were no other lines to worry about, and that made everything much easier.

As I played the carp the rain was still pouring down, and I thought that it would make taking the photos much more difficult.

'Don't be stupid, Steve' I said to myself. 'You haven't even landed the fish yet. Just concentrate on what you're doing, and worry about the photos afterwards. There'll be no photos to take, if you lose it.'

So I played the carp very carefully, and about five minutes later, a lovely mirror carp slid over the net cord. I could see that it was a big fish, probably about mid-thirties, and I punched the air with delight. I had pretty much convinced myself that I wasn`t going to catch any more carp this session, so to catch this fish was a real bonus.

I wet the sling, zeroed the scales, and I set up the camera on the tri-pod, ready to take the photos, but then the rain became even heavier, so I put a cloth over the camera to keep it dry, and went back into the bivvy to shelter from the rain again. I could see a break in the clouds on the horizon, and I hoped that it would stop raining soon, but ten minutes later it still hadn`t stopped. I was undecided what to do now. I could have weighed the fish and sacked it until the weather improved, but I was loath to put it into a sack. It was quite a big fish, and if I sacked it for a while, it would recover its strength and be more lively on the mat, so I preferred to take the photos sooner, rather than later.

'Please stop, just for five minutes' I pleaded, but the rain just kept on coming.

Eventually the rain eased just a little, so I decided to bite the bullet, and take the photos in the light rain. I put the carp in the sling which I placed on the scales on my weighing tri-pod, and watched the dial settled on 36 lbs.2 oz. Fortunately, as I took the carp back to the mat for the photos, the rain stopped and the sun peaked through the clouds a little, so I was able to take the photos in the dry.

I put both hook-baits back into position near to the far bank, and I had just casted the second rod when the heavens opened again. During the afternoon there were several more heavy showers, with short warm sunny periods between them, but the only sounds from my alarms were caused by coots picking up the hook-baits yet again.

I was moving to Argoeuves in the morning, which I was really looking forward to, and because I`d not caught any fish at all during the night this session, I decided to take out the rods, and pack them away just before dark. With the rods already packed, it would take me less time to pack the car in the morning, and I`d be able to get to Argoeuves a lot earlier.

CHAPTER THIRTEEN –
ARGOEUVES IN SEPTEMBER

When I arrived at Argoeuves the wind was blowing across the lake, straight towards the cave, which was the swim that I'd fished the previous month, and it seemed to be the ideal place to be now. Unfortunately, although there was only one other angler fishing at the lake, they were in the swim that I wanted, so I was forced to have a re-think. In the end I set up in the near lawn swim, which meant that I could get my car behind my bivvy, so at least I wouldn't have to use my barrow to get my tackle to the swim.

I put some boilies to soak in a bucket of lake-water for a couple of hours, and then I set up the bivvy and started to make myself comfortable. A few minutes later Claude arrived, and he asked if he could fish with me.

'It would be nice to have some company' I said, and after chatting for ten minutes or so, he set up his bivvy a few yards along the bank from mine.

I then got out the marker rod and soon found three spots that I was happy with. The first two were at about 60 yards range in twelve feet of water, and the third was a little nearer at about 55 yards range, where it was about ten feet deep. I baited the left-hand two spots heavily with boilies, and then spodded a bed of bait over the third. The spod mix was mainly hemp and pellets, but I also put some sweetcorn, chopped tigernuts plus some chopped and whole boilies into the mix too.

With the spots baited and the rods all clipped up, I could relax, and I was sitting in my bivvy when Dupont, the 'garde de pêche', arrived with some very bad news. He told me that this lake, together with the lake across the rod, were both to be used for a 3-day carp match, starting on Wednesday, so I would have to leave in the morning. The match was the French championships for the police and the firemen. I pleaded with Dupont, and said that I'd come all of the way from England to fish here, but it was all to no avail. Claude said that he hadn't realised that there was a carp match planned, and like me, he had thought that by arriving on a Tuesday, it would be nice and quiet.

I was devastated. I had been looking forward to fishing at Argoeuves so much, after the fantastic time that I'd had there in August, and now my plans were in tatters. My only option seemed to be to go to Loeuilly in the morning, or perhaps back to Contre, but packing up and moving again, just for two days fishing, seemed like a lot of effort for little reward.

Half an hour later Dupont returned, and he told me that he had spoken to a member of the committee, who had given him permission to allow me to stay, despite the match, because I'd come so far to fish there.

That was great news, but unfortunately the story didn't end there. When the organiser of the match heard about this, he was not happy, and he complained to the committee, who were forced to reverse their decision to let me stay, so I would have to leave in the morning after all. Dupont apologised and said that he had tried as hard as he could, but there was nothing else that he could do. Claude was very upset too, and he gave the match organiser a piece of his mind. I thought that they were going to come to blows at one point, but fortunately common sense prevailed.

Dupont then had another idea. He said that there was a lake at Glisy, and that I was welcome to fish there if I wanted. This lake was about twenty miles away, and he drove me there in his car, while Claude watched my tackle. When we arrived at Glisy, Dupont showed me around the lake, which was stunning, and told me quite a bit about it. Apparently the lake contained a good head of carp, including a common of over twenty kilos, which is about mid-forties in pounds. Perhaps my trip to Argoeuves wasn`t going to be such a disaster after all, because it seemed that I`d found another gem of a water.

Dupont drove me back to Argoeuves where Benoit was waiting to see me, and the four of us, Claude, Benoit, Dupont and myself, then talked for half an hour or so, until Benoit said that he had to go home for his evening meal. Claude said that he was going to pack up and go home too. He didn`t think that it was worth fishing for just the one night, especially as he would have to leave early the next morning. Dupont went home too, but he promised to come to see me at Glisy the following afternoon.

When the others had gone, I went back to my bivvy, to finish making my rigs for the night. With everything that had happened that afternoon, by the time that I`d made my first cast, it was twenty to seven in the evening. I casted my second rod and then picked up my third, but I didn`t get a chance to cast it, because before I`d even tied on the rig, I heard my middle delkim scream. That hook-bait could only have been in the water for ten minutes at the most, but already I was into a carp. The fish gave me a terrific scrap, kiting well to my left, over the line from my left-hand rod, but fortunately it passed over the other line without giving me any problems. I was then able to continue playing the fish well down the bank to my left, and about fifteen minutes later I lifted the net around a nice mirror. The fish weighed 33 lbs.12 oz. and after I`d photographed it; I watched it swim away strongly.

It was almost eight o`clock before I finally casted my third rod, and 45 minutes later it was dark. It was a mild night without a breath of wind, and just after dark I heard several carp crash out, although most of them seemed to be over towards the far bank, rather than near where I'd positioned my hook-baits. It was encouraging though, and I was optimistic that I might catch another carp before daybreak.

At twenty to eleven that night, my left-hand delkim brought me racing out of my bivvy. Unfortunately when I reached the rod I could see that the hanger had dropped right back to the ground, and a little while later I landed a bream, which didn't please me at all.

It started raining heavily at about half past two the next morning, so I put on some light waterproofs, and I was glad I did when at just after four o'clock the next morning my middle delkim screamed and I ran out into the pouring rain. It was another very strong fish, but I took my time and eventually landed my second carp of the session which was another mirror of 35 lbs.6 oz. this time. It was still dark, so I slipped the carp into a sack, which I placed in the margin, so that I could take some decent pictures at first light.

Luckily the rain stopped for a short time just as it got light, so I was able to take the photos in the dry, and they turned out quite well. I grabbed a bite to eat and a cup of coffee, and then it was time to pack up and head to Glisy.

Despite only fishing for about twelve hours, I was very pleased with the two carp that I'd caught at Argoeuves, and I hoped that I catch a few more at Glisy.

CHAPTER FOURTEEN – GLISY

When I arrived at Glisy on Wednesday morning it was pouring with rain. As I walked to the swim that Dupont had recommended the previous afternoon, I could see several patches of bubbles on the surface, about thirty or forty yards from the bank, which was very encouraging. There was just one other angler there, and he was using a pole to catch small fish. I had a quick word with him and we both cursed the foul weather. When I told him that I was fishing for carp, he told me that there were some very big carp in this lake, although I realised that what may be considered to be a big carp by a pole angler, may not necessarily be considered to be a big carp by a carp angler. I t was another positive comment about the lake however, and Dupont had told me that there was a mid-forty common in the lake.

Now that is a big carp.

I set the bivvy up as soon as I could, and then slowly transferred my tackle from the car to the bivvy, trying to keep it dry as I did so. The rain stopped a couple of times during the morning, but not for long, and it was soon pouring down again. I put some boilies to soak in a bucket of lake-water and then set up the marker rod. I had a rough idea where I wanted to place my baits, which was where I`d seen most of the bubbles.

It had to be a good starting point.

Just as I was chopping up some tigernuts, ready to bait up when I`d found a suitable spot, Dupont came walking along the bank to see me. He`d come to make sure that I`d found the lake and was ok. We talked about the lake for a while, and I showed him the photos of the two mirrors that I`d caught at Argoeuves. He left shortly afterwards to go back to work, but he promised to come back to see me the next day, to see how I'd done.

When I first casted my marker into the lake, I must admit that I was rather disappointed. I casted it about 5 yards from the left-hand tree-line, and I discovered that it was only about two and a half feet deep there. Not only that, but the lake-bed was covered by a lot of dead and rotting leaves, and it didn't look like a good place to put a bait at all. I had a few more casts in the area, and eventually found a spot about ten yards from the tree-line which was three feet deep. The lake-bed was slightly clearer here, but there was still a lot of leaf litter. I catapulted a lot of hemp, pellets and chopped tigers onto the spot, as well as quite a few boilies, and I hoped that perhaps the carp would clear the spot for me, just a little.

I found a better spot for my middle rod, nearer to the centre of the lake, where it was about four feet deep and the lake-bed was a lot clearer, and I baited here very heavily with boilies.

I then struggled to find a spot for my right-hand rod. Most of the area was three and a half feet deep, which wasn't too bad, but once again the lake-bed was covered with dead and rotting leaves. After trying in vain for over half an hour to find a clear area, I decided that the only thing for it was to fish with my hook-bait inside a solid pva bag of boilie crumb, which should give me a reasonable presentation, despite of all of the leaves. Once again I baited here very heavily with boilies and then sat down to tie some rigs.

I decided to use a pop-up on my left-hand rod, and a snowman on my right-hand rod, inside a small pva bag of boilie crumb. I hoped that both of these would be presented reasonably well, despite of all of the rubbish on the bottom. I would use a critically-balanced bottom-bait on the middle rod, where the lake-bed was much clearer.

The rain finally stopped at about four o`clock that afternoon, and I casted my hook-baits for the first time. I sat and watched the water, but there was far less bubbling in the swim, than there had been earlier. I hadn`t actually seen a single carp show, which surprised me, and I was now wondering just how good this lake really was. I had been told that the lake contained a good head of carp, but surely I should have seen some of them, especially considering how shallow it was. The fish couldn`t be far from the surface in that shallow water, but I hadn`t seen any.

It was dark at twenty to nine that evening, and I was starting to wonder if I was going to suffer a blank on my first visit to Glisy, but just five minutes after dark, my right-hand delkim screamed. I picked up the rod and was delighted to feel the heavy weight of a carp, and I carefully eased it away from the snags. The fish didn`t do a lot, it just plodded around slowly, but it was obviously a very strong fish, so I took my time and a few minutes later a very good common slid over the net cord. I shone my torch into the net and could see that it was a superb fish of well over 30 lbs. When I carried it to the mat however, I realised that it was quite a bit bigger than that, and the scales recorded a weight of 39 lbs.7 oz. which was just 9 ounces short of a forty. Just a few minutes earlier I had been quite down, thinking that I might even blank, but now I was absolutely buzzing after catching such a beautiful fish. I put the carp in a sack, which I placed in the margin, so that I could take the photos in the morning. My only worry was that it might be very lively after being sacked up for a few hours and I hoped that it would allow me to lift it up for the camera without beating me up too much.

At about half past ten, I was just thinking of going to bed, when I had a take on my left-hand rod. I was able to bring the fish towards me without too much trouble, but then it charged about in front of me for quite some time. I had caught a glimpse of it in the light of my head-torch, and it didn`t look very big, but no-one told the fish that, and it didn`t want to give up, so it was with some relief that I was able to net it at last. It was another common, a little scamp of 12 lbs.4 oz. but it had given me a terrific fight, and probably gave me more trouble than the big common, which was more than three times its size.

The rest of the night didn`t produce any more carp for me, and I woke at first light the next morning to find it raining again. Fortunately it was only a shower, and by the time that I`d drunk my first cup of coffee of the day, it had stopped. It looked as though it should stay dry for a while now, so I reeled in the rods and started to organise the camera etc. ready to take the photos of the big common.

Despite being sacked overnight, the carp behaved reasonably well on the mat, so I soon had the photos taken and the carp was returned safely to the lake, hopefully to give some other lucky angler a treat, at some time in the future.

I had left some boilies soaking in a bucket of lake-water overnight and I decided to introduce some of these into the swim. To make sure that I put them tight to where I was fishing, I simply tied an empty spod onto the lines of the rods that I was using. These lines were marked with pole elastic and clipped-up for distance, so when I casted the spod into the lake, it landed exactly over my spots, and I was then able to catapult the boilies accurately around it, using it as a marker. The empty spod caused virtually no disturbance, and I thought that it was a far better method than using a marker rod.

I catapulted about fifty boilies around each spot, and then I started to make the rigs that I was going to use that day. I decided to use a tigernut snowman on my left-hand rod, because I`d put quite a lot of chopped tigers in the feed that I had used on that spot. I would use critically-balance baits in small pva bags of boilie crumb on the other two rods. The big common had fallen to a bait fished in a pva bag of boilie crumb, albeit on a snowman, so it seemed like a good idea.

I casted the first rod, but then it started to rain again, so I sat in the bivvy to wait for it to stop, before casting the other two rods, because I didn`t want the pva bags to get wet. The pva bags were meant to dissolve in the lake, and I didn`t want them to dissolve on the bank. It was only a shower and about fifteen minutes later the rain stopped, so I was able to cast the last two rods in the dry.

About ten minutes later another angler arrived. His name was Alain, and he said that he was going to fish the night, so I`d have some company. He set up to my right, but although he was a very nice chap, I`m not sure that his use of a wooden mallet to bang in his bivvy pegs, or the loud splash that the large leads that he was using made as they hit the water, did our chances of catching any more carp much good.

Dupont arrived at about two o`clock that afternoon, and the three of us stood there talking and watching the lake. I showed Dupont the photo of my big carp on my camera, and he said that he was very pleased for me. Before he left to go back to work, he wished me a good journey home, and promised to come to see me when I returned in October.

The wind changed direction completely that afternoon, and it started to blow from the north, so I hoped that we didn`t get any more rain, because the wind would be blowing it straight into the front of my bivvy. The last thing that I wanted was to have to zip the bivvy door shut again, but luckily it stayed dry, so there wasn`t a problem.

Just after four o`clock that afternoon, two people came walking along the bank towards me. They introduced themselves as the president of the association and his wife. The president had heard about me not being able to fish at Argoeuves because of the carp match, after I had driven all the way from England, and he had come to apologise to me personally.

What a wonderful gesture!

They were very nice people, and we talked for some time. In fact we got on so well that they said that they would come to see me again, the next time that I came to Glisy or Argoeuves. Both Dupont and the president had been so friendly and helpful to me, and I`m sure that we will remain friends for many years to come.

As the night approached, the wind dropped, leaving the surface of the lake completely calm once again, but we still didn`t see any signs of carp at all. It had been the same the previous night, but that had changed as soon as it became dark. I just hoped that the same thing would happen tonight.

Surprisingly, the carp didn`t wait until the night this time, and half an hour before dark I had a take on my middle rod. The fish immediately kited to my right, and I was forced to move along the bank, and past my right-hand rod, to follow it. The fight then took place with me standing in the small area between my right-hand rod and a large tree, which made it quite difficult because the carp was determined not to give in, but eventually Alain was able to lift the net around the fish. It was a small mirror of 15 lbs.14 oz. and I was pleased to catch it after not seeing a carp all day. This fish had taken a double critically-balanced bottom-bait in a small pva bag of boilie crumb, and was the first fish that I had taken on my middle rod. Alain took a couple of photos for me, and although he wasn`t used to using my camera, with a little bit of coaching from me, he managed ok.

It was just getting dark as I re-casted the rod. There was no wind at all, but there was a clear sky, and it was starting to feel a lot colder, so it wasn`t long before I was back in my bivvy and inside my sleeping bag in the warm.

About an hour later I was out of my bivvy again once more, to help Alain, who had hooked his first fish of the session, and I netted a small mirror for him of about the same size as my last fish.

There was then not a sound from either of our alarms for some time, and I was fast asleep when I was woken by a take on my left-hand rod. Alain had heard my alarm and was soon standing beside me with the net. This time I had no problems at all with the fish, and I was soon able to guide it over the waiting net. It was another small fish, a common of 11 lbs.10 oz. which had taken a pop-up.

It was only two or three hours until day-light, and I decided not to re-cast the rod. The other two were still in position however, so I hoped that I might still have a chance of another carp, before I left in the morning. It wasn`t to be however, and that proved to be my last fish of the session.

When I reeled in the rods at half past seven the next morning I was very happy with my first session at Glisy. I had caught four fish in my two days there, and although three of them were small, the big common was a fabulous fish. I felt that I`d learnt a lot about the lake in my short time there, and hoped that I`d be able to put that knowledge to good use, when I fished at Glisy again in October, but first I would

spend three days at Argoeuves, and I couldn`t wait to get
back there.

CHAPTER FIFTEEN – BACK TO ARGOEUVES

I arrived at Argoeuves at twenty past seven in the morning, on Monday 5th October. It was still dark, so I rang Anita to let her know that I`d arrived safely, and then I sat in my car waiting for it to get light. By half past seven it was light enough to have a look around the lake, and I was pleased to see that I was the only angler on the bank. I didn`t see any signs of carp and there was no wind at all to help me locate them, so I chose the near lawn swim, where I`d fished the previous time. I`d only spent about twelve hours in the swim in September, but I`d managed to catch two good carp, so I was hoping to catch a few more, now that I was able to fish there for three full days.

I put some boilies into a bucket with some lake-water to soak, and then I set up the bivvy. I knew roughly where to place my hook-baits, so a few quick casts with a marker rod soon found the spots, and I started to introduce some bait. I baited heavily with the soaked boilies on all three areas, but I also spodded a bed of bait onto the right-hand spot. The spod mix that I used was very simple – I just used hemp, chopped tigernuts and peanuts. I spodded a full bucket of this mix out into the lake, which took quite some time, and then I rested the swim while I made myself something to eat and drink. As I was doing this, two other anglers arrived, and one of them fished to my right, while the other set up on the opposite bank.

Just before I was ready to make my first cast it started to rain.

Sods law!

It wasn`t very heavy rain, but it made it difficult for me to keep the pva dry. I managed to get the hook-baits into position, but when I looked at the sky, I could see that the rain was here to stay, and it didn`t stop all afternoon. There was a lot more bird-life on the lake than I`d ever seen before, both coots and ducks, and although they weren`t diving on my baits, they were making a lot of noise as they splashed about chasing each other. I`m was sure that it probably didn`t bother the fish, but I definitely would have preferred a little bit of peace and quiet.

I had planned to re-cast my rods at about six o`clock that evening, and I had tied and baited some new rigs, ready to do just that, but when six o`clock arrived, it was accompanied by even heavier rain, so I decided to leave the rods as they were, but I did catapult some more boilies around the spots.

My friend Benoit arrived at half past six, and as we sat in my bivvy talking and sheltering from the rain, I had a take on my middle rod. I didn`t connect with the fish, and I couldn`t understand why, until I inspected the rig and I saw a piece of mussel-shell on the hook. I think that the mussel-shell must have prevented the hook from penetrating, and I could only put it down to bad luck, so I tied on a new rig, and casted it back into position.

At twenty past ten that night I had a take on my left-hand rod. I hurried out of my bivvy into the rain, and saw that the hanger had dropped back, so I had a fairly good idea what was responsible, and my fears were confirmed when I landed a bream. I re-casted the rod as quickly as possible, and I got back into my sleeping-bag, in the dry.

I was soon fast asleep, but I was woken again less than two hours later when I had another take, on my left-hand rod again. Once again it was a drop-back, and I was soon unhooking another bream. I decided to use a pop-up on that rod for the rest of the night, hoping that it would help me to avoid any more bream, because I`d had quite enough of the slimy pests. I don't enjoy catching bream at the best of times, but in the middle of the night in the pouring rain, I enjoy it even less.

I heard nothing more from my delkims for the rest of the night, and I woke at first light the next morning to find that it was still raining, and if anything the rain was heavier than ever. The rain makes everything rather uncomfortable, and of course it makes the use of pva more difficult, but that wasn't my main concern. I had brought the bait that I was going to use at Glisy, frozen in a cool-box, and it was now starting to thaw, so I needed to dry it. Normally I just hang the air-dry bags on my weighing tri-pod, but in the rain that wasn't possible, so I wouldn't be able to dry the bait properly and I was afraid that the damp boilies would start to deteriorate very quickly.

At ten o'clock my friend Claude arrived, and he set up his bivvy next to mine, so that we could fish together for the next couple of days. We had a quick moan about the terrible weather, and I told him that I'd only caught two bream so far, and no carp at all, which was very disappointing. About half an hour later however, the rain stopped at last, the sky cleared, and soon the sun was shining out of a blue sky, so we both began to feel much better.

'I brought the sun with me.' Claude said, and we both laughed.

With this spell of better weather, I took the opportunity to re-cast all the rods and to introduce some more bait, and then happy with what I'd done, I hung my boilies to dry in the sun. That was a big relief, and now I knew that my bait for Glisy would be fine.

Early that afternoon, I walked to the entrance to put some rubbish into the bin, and I saw a bivvy set up at the end of the lake, but I thought little more of it until I noticed that it was my friend Clément. Clément and I used to fish together several years ago at Conty, but we had only met once since, at the enduro at Loeuilly in April. It was good to see my friend again, and we chatted for a while, before wishing each other 'Bonne Peche', and I returned to my swim.

I wasn`t expecting any action, not during the day anyway, so it was quite a surprise when I heard my right-hand delkim just after two o`clock that afternoon. When I looked at the rod I saw that the hanger had dropped back, so I thought that it was probably another bream, or perhaps one of the many coots that had been diving incessantly, but then the hanger started to rise to the rod-butt and the line pinged out of the clip. I picked up the rod and was immediately forced to back-wind as the carp powered away from me. It`s initial run must have taken at least forty or fifty yards of line from my reel, and it took me a long time before I was able to gain even half of that back onto the spool. It felt like a very big fish, and when it started to kite to my right I had no alternative other than to follow it along the bank, and then I continued to play the fish about fifty yards to the right of my swim. Claude was soon by my side with the net and we were joined by seven or eight other anglers who had come to have a look at the lake, prior to the next enduro, which would take place on Friday, so they all gathered around to watch. It has always amazed me just how hard these Argoeuves carp fight, and this one was no exception. I think it might be due to the deep water, but whatever the reason, this carp certainly didn`t want to give in, and my arm was really aching before Claude was able to lift the net around the fish.

It was a lovely mirror carp of 34 lbs.6 oz. and although it was not quite as big as I had thought it might be whilst I was playing it, I was delighted to have caught it all the same. Claude took the photos for me, and then we watched as the fish swam strongly away, out into the lake again.

The carp had picked up a snowman rig which I had positioned over the spodded area, and I hoped that it was the first of several carp that I would catch from that spot, but whether I caught any more carp from there or not, I had already decided to spod some more hemp and chopped tigers onto the spot the next morning.

I re-casted the rods at five o'clock that evening, two using snowman rigs like the one that had been successful that afternoon, and the other with a double balanced bottom-bait. I catapulted some more boilies over all three spots, and then I went back to my bivvy to get something to eat.

Once again the night was very quiet, but this time even the bream didn't seem to want my baits, so when I woke at first light the next morning, I was rather disappointed that I hadn't caught any more carp. The coots were out in force and one of them found my right-hand hook-bait at about eight o'clock. I cursed them and questioned their parentage, but decided not so re-cast that rod for a while. I would put on a new hook-bait and re-cast the rod later. I made myself the first coffee of the day and then walked the few yards to Claude's swim, to see how he had fared overnight. He said that he hadn't heard a single bleep from his alarms all night, and we both wondered why the carp were being so un-cooperative. Perhaps it was because the lake had been fished a lot lately.

As we stood there talking, I heard one of my delkims, so I hurried back to my swim where I saw that the hanger on my left-hand rod was tight to the butt, and when I lifted the rod I was pleased to find myself connected to another carp at last. Initially I was able to bring the fish towards me without too much trouble, but the closer I brought it to the bank, the harder it fought. The carp then kited to my right, across the line on my middle rod, and I saw the hanger on that rod start to rise and the delkim screamed.

Just what I didn't want to happen.

I loosened the clutch on that reel and asked Claude to lift the rod, to raise the line, hoping that it wasn't too badly tangled. Fortunately when Claude did this, the two lines separated, and I was able to continue playing the carp without any further problems.

The fish was still fighting hard and it was some time before I was able to bring it to the surface, where I saw that it was a common this time. It still wouldn't give in and every time that I brought it towards the waiting net it turned and powered away again, but each time the fish was gradually weakening, and finally Claude was able to lift the net around it.

The carp weighed 31 lbs.4 oz. and Claude took the photos for me again, but that was not as easy as we expected. It was overcast and I placed the mat ready for the photos, but just as I was about to lift the fish, the sun came out and shone from my left-hand side. Now that wouldn't produce good photos at all, so I re-positioned the mat so that the sun was now behind the camera, but unfortunately my car and my bivvy were now in the background, which I didn't want. Luckily the sun then disappeared behind a cloud, so I placed the mat back into its original position, and Claude was finally able to take the photos.

I re-casted the rods at ten o'clock that morning, all with different hook-baits. I used a snowman rig on the left-hand rod, a pop-up on the middle rod, and tigernuts on the third. I just hoped that the carp would take a liking to one of those. I catapulted a couple of dozen boilies over each hook-bait and then reached for my spod rod, which I used to deposit hemp and chopped tigers over my right-hand spot. That was the position that I had spodded a bed of bait over when I had arrived, and it had accounted for my first carp, so I hoped that this might encourage some more fish to feed.

During the afternoon the coots were a nightmare, constantly diving and picking up my hook-baits. They seemed to be attracted to the pop-up, which had been soaked in dip, far more than to either the snowman or the tigernuts. This surprised me because the snowman, with its white top bait, was far more visual, but they definitely preferred the pop-up. It must have been the dip that I'd soaked it in that they found so attractive, and I thought that it might be a good idea to try it at Glisy, when I went there the next day. I had not been bothered by coots at all, when I fished there in September, and there weren't many bream in the lake, so the extra attraction might help me to catch a carp or two.

It was certainly worth a try.

Because of the problems that I was having with the coots, I decided to delay re-casting the rods and baiting up, until just before dark. I would have liked to have everything in place much sooner, because just before dark was a good time for a bite, but I doubted that the coots would leave my hook-baits undisturbed, so it just wasn't worth the hassle.

Two of my hook-baits would be snowman rigs using a white spice top bait. The coots didn't seem to like those as much, so I hoped that they might be left alone for long enough to give the carp a chance to find them. On the other rod I would use double balanced bottom-baits, which is what I'd caught the common on, so all in all I felt that I'd done all that I could. I wouldn't use much free bait that night, just a few boilies around each hook-bait. I had introduced a lot of bait during the last couple of days, and although the coots had mopped up a lot of it, I was sure that the carp would still be attracted to the area.

I hoped so anyway.

I was just casting my last rod when my friend Patrice arrived. Clément had phoned him to let him know that I was at Argoeuves, and Patrice had driven all the way from Conty to see me. We drank some coffee and talked for an hour or so, and then he left to go back home.

It was well after dark by now, so I was soon inside my sleeping-bag in the warm, but I wasn't there long because at just before nine o'clock one of my delkims screamed, and I was soon making my way out of the bivvy towards the flashing LED. It was my right-hand rod, but the hanger had dropped back to the ground, just like a bream-bite, and sure enough I was soon reeling in another of the slimy pests.

I took the rod back to my bivvy, to get it ready to make another cast, but before I could do that, my left-hand delkim started screaming for attention.

'Not another bream.' I thought, but this time it wasn't a drop-back, the hanger was tight to the spool on my reel was clicking, so I realised that it must be a carp. The fight was slow and ponderous, and I didn't have a lot of trouble bringing the carp towards me, where Claude did the honours with the net. When we parted the mesh I got a real surprise. I was expecting to see a relatively small carp, but what I saw in the light of my head-torch was a mirror carp of very close to forty pounds staring back at me. The scales showed a weight of 38 lbs.14 oz. and I then carefully sacked the fish so that we could take some decent photos at first light. That was my third carp of over thirty pounds for the session, and they were the only three fish that had been caught whilst I had been there, so I must have been doing something right, so I re-casted the rods and then got back into my sleeping-bag with a smile on my face.

A couple of hours later I was out of the bivvy again to do battle with my fourth carp of the session. It was another common this time, but was smaller than the other fish at just 24 lbs.8 oz. and I released it without bothering with a photo.

Just before light the next morning I caught another bream on my right-hand rod, but that proved to be my last fish of the session. Claude helped me with the photos of the mirror, and despite it having been sacked overnight, it behaved quite well on the mat and we were soon able to return it to the lake, and watch it swim away safely.

I took the rods out at half past eight that morning and started packing up, ready for the move to Glisy. I had caught four carp during my three days at Argoeuves, three of which had been over thirty pounds, which was a very good result in what had been quite difficult conditions, and I hope that I could achieve something equally as good at Glisy over the next three days.

CHAPTER SIXTEEN – GLISY AGAIN

I arrived at Glisy just after midday and I noticed a bivvy on the first part of the lake, on the right of the road, but when I arrived at the main part of the lake I was pleased to see that there was no-one there. I took my time and looked carefully at several swims, but I didn`t see any signs of fish at all. The last time that I`d fished here I`d seen a lot of bubbling, as the carp gave their presence away, but this time there was nothing, so I decided to fish in the same swim as before. At least I had a good idea where to place my hook-baits in this swim. I had intended to cast to the areas where I saw most bubbling, but there was nothing to help me at all.

I set up the bivvy, made myself comfortable, and then baited up three spots.

Two of these spots were baited quite heavily with boilies, but on the other spot, where I would cast my left-hand rod, I put a lot of hemp, pellets and chopped tigernuts, in addition to the boilies. After I`1d baited up, I left the swim to recover, with no lines in the water for quite some time, and I finally casted my hook-baits into position at just after six o`clock that evening. There was now only about an hour or so until dusk, and I sat there with my eyes glued to the lake, hoping to see some signs of carp, but I still saw nothing at all.

It was quite cool after dark, and I was soon inside my sleeping bag in the warm, but I wasn`t tired so I lay there reading. At about nine o'clock I heard my delkim scream for attention, and I hurried out of my bivvy towards the flashing LED. When I picked up the rod I was a little unsure what I was attached to. The fish felt quite small, and a few seconds later I was amazed to see a bream come sliding across the surface towards me. Dupont had told me that there were virtually no bream in the lake, and Patrice had said that he`d always used very small hook-baits at Glisy because there wasn`t a problem with nuisance fish.

They were both wrong because there was definitely at least one bream in the lake, and I`d just caught it.

I tied up a new rig with another pva bag of boilie crumb, and casted it back out into the lake, but even that didn`t go according to plan. I somehow managed to leave the cast a little short, and it didn`t hit the clip, so I had to cast it again. Of course, because I was using a pva bag, this meant drying everything off, and then tying up a new pva bag, before I could make the cast. Fortunately my second attempt was much better, and it landed perfectly, exactly where I wanted it. Because the lake at Glisy is so shallow, the last thing that I wanted was to make too many casts, and to cause too much disturbance, so not hitting the clip with my first attempt annoyed me even more than it normally would have done, but I only had myself to blame.

About an hour later my right-hand rod was disturbed by a bream once again, but this time I didn`t bother to re-cast it. Being constantly woken to deal with bream during the night didn`t seem like a good idea to me, so I went back to the bivvy to get some sleep.

At twenty to four the next morning I had a take on my middle rod, and this time I realised that it was definitely a carp. It didn`t feel like a very big fish, but I took my time and I soon had a small common in the net. The carp weighed 16 lbs.3 oz. but it was a stunning little fish, and I was delighted to be off the mark. I sacked it up so that I could take some photos in daylight, which wasn`t that far away, and then I re-casted the rod, using the same hook-bait as before, because it still looked fine. I`d caught that fish by using a two critically-balanced bottom-baits with a small stringer, and I was beginning to think that perhaps that was a better approach for this lake than using pva bags of boilie crumb. The bream found the boilie crumb far too attractive for my liking, and I wanted my hook-baits to stay in place for long enough, so that a carp could find them.

I had no more action that night and I woke at first light on Friday morning to find the lake flat calm and without any signs of carp at all. I took some photos of the common and then baited up the three spots. I baited all three with quite a lot of boilies, but I also put hemp, pellets and chopped boilies on the left-hand spot once again.

Although I had decided not to use pva bags of boilie crumb during the night again, because of the bream problem, I thought that it might be worth a try during the day, when the fish were much less active, so I used them on all three rods. The hook-baits were the same on all of the rods too – small dumbbell-shaped balanced bottom-baits, wrapped in boilie-paste, on combi D-rigs. Once the hook-baits were all in position, I made myself something to eat, and then tied some rigs ready for the night.

At about four o'clock that afternoon, two other anglers arrived. One of them, who was called Roman, came to introduce himself, and he told me that they were going to fish for the next two nights. They had a look at several swims, but eventually decided to fish about 100 yards to my right. This gave us all plenty of room and ensured that we wouldn't get in each other's way. It's nice to have a bit of company, but I prefer not to be crowded, and their swim choice suited everyone.

If only all anglers were that considerate.

I re-casted the rods for the night at six o'clock that evening, and used the same rigs and hook-baits on each rod – two critically-balanced bottom-baits with a small stringer. I then catapulted about twenty boilies around each one. The first two went in perfectly, but when I catapulted some boilies around the right-hand hook-bait, six ducks appeared from nowhere and started diving. In water that was little more than three feet deep, you can imagine the disturbance that they caused. The ducks had been around when I had introduced some bait both the previous afternoon and that morning, and they hadn`t dived on the baits before, so I don`t know what made them do it this time. I was tearing my hair out in frustration, but then I had an idea. I started to catapult a few boilies just to the right of the ducks, and they moved towards where the boilies were landing, and started to dive there instead. I then catapulted some more boilies even further right, and I was gradually able to lead them away from my swim. That all worked very well, but unfortunately I feared that the damage had already been done.

Friday night was very disappointing indeed and I didn`t catch anything at all, not even a bream. Thinking back over my two visits to Glisy so far, of the five carp that I had caught, three of them were caught by using some sort of attractor as a hook-bait, rather than a natural-looking boilie – two on washed-out pink pop-ups and one on a snowman rig with a white top bait. During the previous night I had used double bottom-baits on all three rods and it hadn`t worked, so perhaps that was a mistake, and I decided to do something different. During the day I would fish different positions, and I casted my left-hand rod nearer to the snag on the east bank. On this rod I used a small dumbbell-shaped balanced bottom-bait with a yellow corn-stop to give it some visual attraction, and I put this inside a small pva bag of boilie crumb. I hoped that this would ensure that the presentation was perfect, and the boilie crumb would also give loads of attraction. I didn`t think that the bream would be a problem during the day, so that didn't bother me at all. I catapulted just eight boilies around the rig.

I casted my middle rod seventy yards towards the gap, with a washed-out pink pop-up on a 360 rig. I hadn't fished at anywhere near that distance here in the past, so I felt that it had to be worth a try. I fished the pop-up as a single hook-bait, without any free-baits near it at all.

My right-hand rod was fished at just five yards range with tigernuts, and I sprinkled a few chopped tigernuts and a handful of hemp around the hook-bait. I had noticed a few bubbles in that area on a couple of occasions during the last two days, and although I couldn't be sure that they were caused by carp, it was more activity than I'd seen over my baited areas, so once again I felt that it was worth a try.

I baited my original positions lightly with just a dozen boilies on each, and left them undisturbed for the rest of the day. Even if my new positions didn't produce a fish for me, at least my baited areas were being rested, which could only help. I would cast my hook-baits to original positions for my last night at Glisy, but perhaps with pop-up's on at least two of the rods. I didn't know if any of these changes would bring me any success, but at least I felt that I had given it my best shot.

The rest of the day didn't produce a single bleep from my delkims and I started to re-cast my rods at six o'clock that evening. I had just got my left-hand rod into position when Fabrice arrived. He was going to try some lure-fishing for perch and pike, and he asked me if I'd seen anything that day. Unfortunately I couldn't help him much because I hadn't seen anything at all, so we wished each other 'Bonne Peche' and he carried on walking around the lake.

I soon had my last two rods in position and I decided not to add any more free-baits at all, because I was sure that there was already plenty out there. I was using washed-out pink pop-up`s on 360 rigs on two of my rods, and two balanced bottom-baits on the middle rod. That hook-bait had been soaked in dip to add extra attraction. We would soon see if my theory about attractor baits being more successful here was correct or not.

It was dark by a quarter to eight that night, but the wind didn`t drop with the coming of darkness as it usually did, and if anything it was even stronger than before.

I lay on my bed-chair and rang Anita, but I had to cut the call short when my sounder box started to bleep. It was my middle rod, but unfortunately the hanger returned to its original position, so I assumed that it was just a line-bite, and I returned to my bivvy to ring Anita back.

I read for a while until I became tired, and then soon fell asleep, but I was woken at twenty past ten when I had a take on my left-hand rod. It was only a small fish, a common of 10 lbs.12 oz. but I hadn`t caught a carp for almost two days, so it was very welcome.

I soon had the hook-bait back in position and I was fast asleep in my sleeping bag when my delkim signalled another take just after midnight, but what followed was just a catalogue of mistakes. When I heard the take, I looked at my sounder box where I saw a green LED flashing, so I knew that it was my right-hand rod, and I hurried towards it, but as I stood by the rod, I couldn`t understand what was happening. I could hear the sounder box still bleeping, but the hanger wasn`t moving at all.

'Perhaps there was something wrong with the alarm' I thought, so I tried moving the hanger, which made the sounder box bleep even more and the alarm seemed perfectly ok. As I stood there, the sounder box kept bleeping periodically, but there was still no movement from the

171

hanger, and I was totally at a loss, as to what was going on, then I glanced to my left and saw the blue LED flashing on my left-hand rod, and I realised my mistake. I had mistaken the blue LED of my left-hand rod, for the green LED of my right-hand rod.

What a plonker!

I hurried along the bank and luckily found that the carp was still attached, so I started to ease it back towards me. Unfortunately, after all that time, the carp had kited to my right, well past my other two lines, and as I brought the carp back towards me, the hanger on my right-hand rod pulled up tight to the rod-butt and the delkim started bleeping, as the two lines came together. I kept trying to bring the carp towards me, and luckily the fish came clear of that line after a short while, only to then pick up the line on my middle rod. Once again the hanger pulled up tight and the delkim started to scream. After about a minute or so, the carp came clear of that line too, and at last I was able to play the fish without any more problems, or so I thought until I bent down to pick up the landing net, only to discover that it wasn`t there. It was over by my right-hand rod, where I`d gone when I`d first heard my alarm. I was fishing with my rods well spread out along the bank and there was a tree over-hanging the margin between myself and the landing net, which was thirty yards to my right along the bank, so I had a real problem. There was no way that I could get the fish to the net, because I couldn`t get the line past the tree, so there was only one thing that I could do, which was to loosen the clutch on the reel, put down the rod, and run to get the net. To my amazement, when I returned the fish was still attached, and I was able to play it back towards me and lift the net around it.

I really didn't deserve that fish, but you know what they say – 'It's better to be lucky than to be good'.

It was another small common, a little bigger than the last at 12 lbs.13 oz. The hook-baits on both of my other rods had been dragged out of position, so I had to re-cast all three rods, and it was quite some time before I was able to get back into my nice warm sleeping bag once again.

At just before half past six, I was woken once more by a screaming take to my middle rod. There was no warning bleep, it just screamed off. I was in a deep sleep at the time, and as I got out of bed, still in a daze, I dropped my head-torch onto the floor and then struggled to get my boots on. The more I tried to hurry, the more I struggled, but eventually I was out of my bivvy with the rod in my hands. Fortunately it was the middle rod this time which was being fished into open water, so my delay in reaching the rod didn't cause a problem. I eased the carp back towards me, but it took quite some time because it fought very strongly, but after a few more minutes I was able to guide the fish over the waiting net. It was a mirror this time and at nineteen pounds exactly, it was the biggest fish of the session.

I was soon back asleep, but it seemed as though I had only just closed my eyes when the alarm on my phone started to ring. I had set the alarm for first light, and it was time for me to get out of bed, because I soon had to start packing away my kit, ready to start the long journey home. I made myself a cup of coffee to wake me up, and then took the photos of the three fish that I'd got sacked up in the margin.

I had caught four carp this time at Glisy and none of them were over twenty pounds in weight, which was rather disappointing, but in the end I was quite pleased with the session. I felt that I'd probably introduced too much bait at the start, but Tim Paisley's disappearing food source theory sprang to mind, and by cutting down the feed and changing some of my hook-baits to make them more visible, I had managed to catch three fish on the last night, which I was very pleased with. I thought that I`d fished quite well – apart from going to the wrong rod of course.

On the long drive home I thought back over what had been a marvellous year for me. I had found two new lakes at Glisy and Argoeuves and had caught some fantastic fish. The biggest was that enormous mirror of 49 lbs.14 oz. from Loeuilly, but I`d also caught a common of over 40 lbs. and a personal best grass carp too, along with a host of other big fish. I`d loved the time I`d spent in France and made some wonderful friends, and they had made the time that I`d spent there just as special as the fish that I`d caught. I`d certainly go back to see them all again, but that would not be until the following spring. I`d spend a lot of time during the winter looking back over the photos of the fish that I`d caught and re-living the memories.

If I enjoyed my time in France next year half as much as I had done over the last twelve months, it would be another very special year.

About The Author

Steve Graham lives in Staffordshire with his wife Anita and his dog Stan. He has two children – Lynne and John, and two grandchildren – Logan and Dylan.

He took early retirement at the age of 53 which has allowed him to spend more time doing the things in life that he enjoys the most, amongst which are of course carp fishing and writing.

At the time of writing this book Steve has been an angler for over fifty years, and for the last twenty-five years his fishing has been almost exclusively for carp. During this time Steve has caught some huge fish, including countless numbers over the magic forty pound mark, both in England and in France.

Steve now does the majority of his fishing in France, but not on the commercial waters that most English anglers fish. Steve prefers the much quieter less well known waters, where there is still a bit of mystery. Despite not being known by the majority of English anglers, these quiet waters still hold some fantastic fish. Steve has also made a lot of good friends on his journeys through France, and they have allowed him to find even more of these lesser known lakes.

I suppose you could say that Steve is living the dream.

Other Books By Steve Graham

From Gudgeon to Carp

This is Steve's first book. It is the story of an angler and the journey through his fishing life, plus all of the adventures along the way. It describes his progression from catching small fish on the canal as a young boy, through many different species of fish, and larger and larger quarry. But all these different fish lead on to the ultimate - Carp.

Although predominantly about angling, this is a book that can be enjoyed by non-anglers too, as page after page reveals all the ups and downs that he experiences in search of his obsession.

Names have been changed to protect the innocent, but the story is almost totally true, or as near as the authors fading memory would allow.

More Carp Fishing

'More Carp Fishing' is Steve's second book and carries on his story from where his first book 'From Gudgeon to Carp' ended. It continues the story of his fishing life and describes the many exciting experiences in his quest for those most elusive of fish – **BIG CARP**.

There are chapters on a real diversity of different waters including two very low stock waters in England, other English syndicate and club waters and also several different venues in France where Steve caught some huge fish. The chapters relating to the largest low stock lake in particular are absolutely gripping. At the outset the stock of carp in the water was totally unknown, which is exciting enough in this day and age. The amount of natural food in the lake was extremely high and the fishing was to prove to be very difficult, but the results were well worth the effort.

Most of the French lakes were not commercial venues and they had that extra spice of the unknown that Steve enjoys so much, but they were also very testing at times. Once again though, the effort was well rewarded with the capture of some spectacular fish.

This book describes the many tremendous highs and also the devastating lows that he experiences in search of his obsession, and also all the people that he has met along the way.

Page after page describes the journey through his fishing life in gripping detail, some parts full of humour, other parts tragic and some filled with pure elation.

Carp Fishing Tips and Theories

Steve's first two books described the journey through his fishing life, but this book is entirely different. It is crammed full of tips and theories which he has accumulated during his fifty years of angling.

The book contains twenty different chapters including two fascinating sections on rigs and hook-baits, and many tips that have seldom been seen in print before. No secrets have been held back and with over 130 pages, the reader cannot fail to find some tips that will help them to put more Carp on the bank.

A Carp Fishing Year

'A Carp Fishing Year' is Steve's fourth book, which continues his carp fishing story from where 'More Carp Fishing' ended. It describes a lot of the fishing that Steve did in France, but not on the easy commercial waters that so many anglers fish, where every carp has a name. Steve much prefers the less well known waters, where there is still a little bit of mystery. The next fish could be a double, or it could be the fish of a lifetime, and that just adds to the excitement.

The book tells of all his successes and failures along the way, including some dramatic highs, when Steve catches some wonderful fish, but also some devastating lows that all true carp fishermen can identify with.

Gone Carp Fishing

This book covers a very exciting period of Steve's fishing life, during which he discovers some fantastic new waters and makes a lot of new friends.

Some of his fishing was done on some very difficult waters and Steve reveals everything that he did that helped him to catch some fantastic carp.

The way Steve writes, the reader almost feels as if they were out there on the bank with him. The book is written with so much emotion and enthusiasm that it must surely inspire anyone reading it to want to pick up a rod and try for themselves.

Carp Fishing Tips and Theories – Book Two

Ever since Steve`s first Tips and Theories book was published, Steve has been bombarded with requests from readers, all asking when he would write a sequel, and here it is – 'Carp Fishing Tips and Theories - Book Two'.

Just like his first Tips and Theories book, this one is crammed full of tips and theories that Steve has accumulated during his many years of fishing. There are more than twenty chapters, each on a different subject, and the readers are sure to find many tips here that will help them to put more carp on the bank.

Steve has also written two books in French – **'Du Goujon À La Carpe'** and **'Pêche À La Carpe'**.

These are translations of Steve`s first two books – **'From Gudgeon To Carp'** and **'More Carp Fishing'**, which Steve has translated into French.

If you would like to know anything about Steve's fishing or the places that he has fished, or if you would like to know about any new books that Steve writes, please send your email address to anita.graham@talktalk.net

In the meantime, enjoy the books and enjoy your fishing.

Lightning Source UK Ltd.
Milton Keynes UK
UKHW011837101218
333768UK00001B/33/P